Anonymous

Delicate Dishes

A cook book

Anonymous

Delicate Dishes
A cook book

ISBN/EAN: 9783744781213

Printed in Europe, USA, Canada, Australia, Japan

Cover: Foto ©Lupo / pixelio.de

More available books at **www.hansebooks.com**

DELICATE DISHES.

A COOK BOOK

Compiled by

LADIES OF ST. PAUL'S CHURCH,

CHICAGO,   .   ILLINOIS.

1896

ENTERED ACCORDING TO ACT OF CONGRESS, IN THE YEAR 1896,
BY W. H. FRENCH,
IN THE OFFICE OF THE LIBRARIAN CONGRESS,
IN WASHINGTON

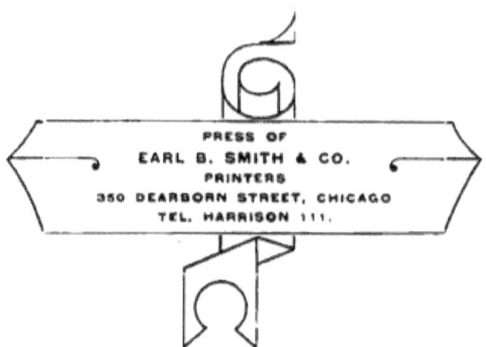

PREFACE.

It is with much pleasure that the ladies of St. Paul Parish commend this little volume to the public's notice.

No claim of originality is made for it. It contains no hitherto unpublished secrets of the culinary art, routed from obscurity by energetic hands, and dusted for our delectation..... Each housekeeper has simply selected a few of her choicest recipes and added them to the collection, that her friends may enjoy with her these "Delicate Dishes." As each one bears the hall mark of the sender's name, no further recommendation need to be added.

The committee in charge wish to thank those without whose prompt and generous co-operation such a book would have been impossible. Each one has given of the best of her store, and given it gladly. With this in remembrance, they feel confident that not only will the collection itself prove a success, but it may be the means of bringing into even warmer and closer relationship those who are bound together by a common interest, and working together for a common cause.

Chicago, Easter 1896.

"There is a knack in doing many a thing,
    Which labor cannot to perfection bring;
Therefore, however great in your own eyes,
    Pray do not hints from other folks despise."

SOUPS.

"A genial savor
Of certain stews; . . . .
Things which in hungry mortals' eyes find favor."

CREAM OF PEA SOUP.

Press 1 can of French peas through a colander. Put 1 quart of milk in double boiler; when boiling, add the peas. Rub one tablespoonful each of butter and flour together, add them to the boiling milk and stir until it thickens. Salt and pepper to taste.

Mrs. B. R. Wells.

CELERY CREAM SOUP.

One quart of rich milk, ¼ cup of flour, 2 heaping teaspoonfuls of celery salt, ½ pint of whipped cream.

Mrs. J. M. Taylor.

CREAM OF CELERY SOUP.

Four pounds of stewing veal, 1 veal soup-bone, 2 tablespoonfuls of salt, ½ teaspoonful of pepper, 1 soup bunch, without celery, 3 small onions, 4 whole cloves, 4 whole allspice, 3 quarts of cold water. Heat slowly and boil gently until reduced one-half. Strain and cool, then remove fat and keep warm. Heat in double boiler 1 quart of milk. Melt in a thick-bottomed pan 4 tablespoonfuls of butter, add 1 large bunch of celery, using the outside only. Brown well, and add 5 tablespoonfuls of flour, mix well and add the hot stock, a pint at a time. Stir until smooth, add enough milk to make the soup creamy, strain and do not boil after the milk is put in.

MRS. GEORGE MEHRING.

CREAM OF CORN SOUP.

One pint of grated corn, cooked in 1 pint of hot water ½ hour. Boil quart of milk and 1 slice of onion, rub 1 heaping teaspoonful of flour with 2 of butter, add a little boiling milk, and when smooth, stir into the milk and onion and cook 8 minutes. Remove the onion, add corn and salt and pepper.

TOMATO BISQUE.

Put 1 quart of milk on to boil. Rub 2 tablespoonfuls of butter, 2 of flour and ½ teaspoonful of soda together. Boil 1 quart can of tomatoes and stir into it the above mixture. Stir until it boils, then add to it the boiling milk, with 1 teaspoonful of salt and 1 of sugar. MRS. RUSSELL H. STEVENS.

SOUPS.

CREAM OF ASPARAGUS SOUP.

Wash and tie up one bunch of asparagus, put it in boiling water and boil gently ¾ hour. Remove, cut off the tips and lay them aside. Put 1 quart of milk on to boil in double boiler, press the stalks through colander and add to the milk. Rub 1 tablespoonful of butter and 2 of flour together, put into the milk and stir constantly until it thickens. Add the asparagus tips, salt and pepper to taste. MRS. M. E. DAYTON.

CREAM POTATO SOUP.

Boil 5 good sized potatoes. Boil 1½ pints of milk and stir into it ¼ pound of butter, a little salt and nutmeg. Mash the potatoes and pour this over them. Stir and strain through a sieve. Stir over the fire until it boils again, pour into tureen over 6 Boston crackers, split and toasted. SELECTED.

TURTLE BEAN SOUP.

One pint of black beans soaked over night in cold, soft water, ½ pound of salt pork, ½ pound of fresh beef, 1 onion, 1 gallon of soft water, 1 grated carrot. Boil until tender, 3 or more hours, strain through colander, return to kettle, add a few cloves, forcemeat balls, sliced lemon, hard-boiled eggs, chopped; salt and pepper. MRS. F. H. RADFORD.

VALENTINES VARNISHES **VALENTINE & COMPANY,** Coach and Car Varnishes and Colors.

BLACK BEAN SOUP.

One quart of black beans, soaked over night. Boil until soft with 2 pounds of beef, pepper and salt, good sized onion, with 3 cloves in it, a little lemon peel. Strain and pour it over 2 hard-boiled eggs, sliced thin, juice of ½ a lemon and a wine glass of sherry wine.

F. C. VAN WYCK.

BOUILLON.

Pour 1 quart of cold water over 2 pounds of lean beef, chopped fine. Let it simmer 4 hours. Strain, cool and stir in the beaten white of 1 egg. Boil until clear, season with salt and white pepper, color with 1 teaspoonful of burnt brown sugar, strain and serve.

MRS. MILLER.

SALSIFY, OR OYSTER PLANT SOUP.

One dozen salsify roots, scraped, sliced and put into one pint of boiling water; boil slowly until tender, add 1 quart of milk 1 tablespoonful of butter, 2 of flour, rubbed together, 6 whole allspice, 1 blade of mace, 1 bay leaf. Stir until it boils. Add salt and pepper, and let it stand ten minutes on the back of the stove. Remove bay leaf and serve.

SELECTED.

VERT PRE.

Cook 1 quart of spinach leaves with a teaspoonful of salt in ½ pint of water for 10 minutes, drain, return

---

"Use Imperial French Poultry Seasoning."

to kettle, add 2 tablespoonfuls of butter, ½ pint of peas, 1 bay leaf, 1 sprig of parsley, 1 small onion and 3 pints of stock. Cook ½ hour, press through sieve and return to kettle. Moisten 2 tablespoonfuls of arrowroot, add, stir, and as soon as it boils add ½ pint of cream, salt and pepper. Serve with fried bread cut in small squares.

CREAM OF CELERY SOUP.

Boil 1 large head of celery in 1 pint of water ¾ hour. Boil 1 pint of milk with 1 large slice of onion, a blade of mace; mix 1 tablespoonful of flour smoothly in a little cold milk and stir into the boiling milk. Mash the celery in the water in which it was cooked, and cook ten minutes longer; then stir it into the boiling milk, add 1 tablespoonful of butter, salt and pepper and serve at once. MRS. E. G. GILBERT.

BISQUE OF OYSTERS.

One quart of fair-sized fresh oysters, 1 quart of rich milk or cream, 8 soda crackers, rolled, a teaspoonful of beef extract, a saucerful of finely minced celery, 2 tablespoonfuls of butter, worked into an equal quantity of flour, the yolks of 3 eggs, salt and pepper to taste, with a sprinkle of cayenne. Chop the oysters, put into stewpan with their own liquor and a pint of water, the celery, beef extract, crackers,

VALENTINE'S VARNISHES VALENTINE & COMPANY, Coach and Car Varnishes and Colors.

salt, pepper and a little parsley. Boil slowly for 20 minutes. Rub through a sieve until all moisture has been pressed through. Return to stove, add milk and simmer again for 10 minutes. Set back and very carefully stir in the beaten yolks of the eggs; serve at once.

CELERY SOUP WITH OYSTERS.

Cut 3 heads of celery into small pieces, using both roots and stalks; add a piece of onion as large as a hickory nut and a sprig of parsley; put into a saucepan with a pint of boiling water and boil ½ an hour; put one quart of milk into a double boiler; rub to a smooth paste a heaping tablespoonful of flour, and add to it, a little at a time, ½ cup of warm milk; pour this into the hot milk and stir until it is smooth and creamy; remove the parsley and rub the remaining contents with water through the colander and add this to the milk; add a teaspoonful of salt and ½ a teaspoonful of pepper; as soon as it boils add 2 dozen nicely washed oysters; when it reaches the boiling point again remove from the fire and serve. C. R. R.

BISQUE OF CLAMS.

Wash and chop 1 quart of clams. Put into a stewpan with ½ pint of white stock (or water), 1 slice of onion, 2 blades of celery, a tiny bit of mace, a bay leaf and a sprig of parsley. Cover; cook gently half an hour. In another saucepan have a pint of stock and a scant pint of stale

---

"Use Imperial French Poultry Seasoning."

bread crumbs. Let this cook very slowly 20 minutes. When the clams have cooked ½ an hour strain the liquor, from them into the pan with the bread crumbs. Stir and rub through a sieve. Return to the fire, add 3 tablespoonfuls of butter and 2 of flour rubbed together, 2 teaspoonfuls of salt, one-third teaspoonful of white pepper, one pint of milk and one of cream (or 2 pints of rich milk) heated to a boiling point. Let it boil up once, strain again and serve. With it pass the

PROFITEROLES.

Into a saucepan put 2 tablespoonfuls of butter and ½ a cup of boiling water. Put on the fire, and when it boils add three-fourths cup of flour, and beat well 2 minutes. Remove from the fire, and when cool break into it 2 eggs; beat for 10 minutes, add one-half teaspoonful of salt, make into balls size of a pea, put them into a slightly buttered pan; bake in a moderate oven 10 minutes.

ANDALUSIAN SOUP.

Three quarts of soup stock, 2 cupfuls of dry stewed tomatoes (if canned tomatoes are used they must be drained before stewing), 1 cupful of minced soup vegetables, mostly onions; 1 small cupful of butter and same of flour. Fry the minced vegetables in the butter, until the latter has

VALENTINE & COMPANY,
Coach and Car Varnishes and Colors.

become a light brown, mix in the flour and set the pan inside the oven for the mixture to brown thoroughly without burning. Then scrape the contents of the pan into the soup stock, throw in 8 cloves, half a bay leaf, a teaspoonful of black pepper; simmer half an hour and strain; add the tomatoes rubbed through a colander and set the soup pot on the back of the stove to slowly boil a half hour longer; skim occasionally. Season with salt. The soup should be of the consistency of thin brown sauce and is delicious enough to pay for the trouble of making.

PIQUANT PEA SOUP.

One pint of green dried peas—or fresh ones. If dried scald in a solution of saleratus water, blanch them thoroughly and cook gently in 2 quarts of water until tender and soft. Pass them through a sieve. Chop 2 onions and fry in 2 tablespoonfuls of butter, add 6 cloves and 1 bay leaf and then stir all together. Put in a tablespoonful of salt and a cup of either canned or whole tomatoes. Let the whole cook very slowly for an hour, when, if it seems too thick, add a little boiling water and let it cook a little longer. Then add a pinch of red pepper and a tablespoonful of butter, and just before serving, a cupful of squares of bread which have been fried brown in butter until of a pretty golden hue. Mrs. Ryan.

"Use Imperial French Poultry Seasoning."

ALMOND SOUP.

One cup of rice, 1 tablespoonful sugar, 5 pints of milk, ½ teaspoonful of salt, ½ pound almonds. Wash the rice, put in a farina boiler with 1 quart of milk. Cook slowly till every grain is tender. While the rice is cooking shell and blanch the almonds, chop very fine and then pound them in a mortar, adding a few drops at a time a half cup of milk, forming a smooth paste. Place the paste with the sugar and remaining quantity of milk in a double boiler and simmer for thirty minutes. When the rice is done turn it carefully into the soup tureen, pour over it the almonds and milk, season with teaspoonful of salt and serve.

R. A. R.

VEGETABLE SOUP.

Take 8 or 10 cupfuls of stock, in which almost any kind of meat has been boiled—the richer the better. Skim off most of the fat. Almost every kind of vegetable can be used. Take a piece of each and cut into dice shapes. Boil the hard vegetables, such as carrots, turnips, onions, celery, etc., together in a pint of water an hour in a little saucepan; drain off the water, put them into the stock and add the easy cooking kinds, such as cauliflowers, potatoes or whatever may be at hand, and simmer ½ hour. At last add a half cup tomatoes, small teaspoonful salt, half tea-

VALENTINE & COMPANY,
Coach and Car Varnishes and Colors.

spoonful pepper and a tablespoonful cornstarch mixed in a cup of cold water. Cook five minutes and serve.

C. E. C.

CAULIFLOWER SOUP.

Select good-sized head of cauliflower. Wash and pick apart. Put in quart of boiling water with teaspoonful of salt and simmer for half hour. Drain and add to the water 1 pint of milk, with a teaspoonful of onion juice and a bay leaf; rub together 1 large tablespoonful of butter, 2 even tablespoonfuls of flour, stir carefully into hot mixture until it comes to boiling point. Add the cauliflower and serve at once.

SPANISH SOUP.

Soak 1 pound of white beans over night, boil them the next morning till tender, add 1 small white cabbage, which has been cut up fine, a bit of bacon, a whole red pepper and some salt; boil the whole for an hour. Heat some lard or drippings in a saucepan and fry in it a sliced onion; put in the soup little by little; stir often with a wooden spoon. A little olive butter and garlic makes this a perfect representative of the favorite soup kept for all travelers in Spanish climes. Selected.

SCOTCH BROTH.

Two pounds scraggy neck of mutton. Cut meat in small pieces and put in soup pot with 2 quarts of water, 1

"Use Imperial French Poultry Seasoning."

turnip, 2 carrots, 1 onion and a stalk of celery, all cut fine Simmer two hours. Cook 1 tablespoonful of flour and 1 of butter together until perfectly smooth; stir in soup, and add a teaspoonful of chopped parsley; season with salt and pepper.

PUREE OF POTATOES.

Boil and mash in 2 quarts of water 4 large potatoes, a small onion, 2 stalks of celery and a sprig of parsley. When done pass through a sieve, return to the fire, add salt and pepper to taste, and 2 generous teaspoonfuls of butter rubbed into one of flour. Boil up once and pour into a soup tureen over a cupful of rich milk.

OATMEAL SOUP.

Two quarts of any meat broth, ½ can tomatoes, 1 medium-sized onion, salt and pepper to taste, a stalk or two of celery (if at hand), 1½ teacupfuls of oatmeal. Put broth, vegetables and seasoning over the fire together and let come to a boil; then throw in the oatmeal and stir smooth. Boil until as thick as cream, then strain through a colander and serve. MISS CAMPBELL.

VALENTINES VARNISHES **VALENTINE & COMPANY,**
Coach and Car Varnishes and Colors.

SALADS AND SAUCES.

"Epicurean cooks sharpen . . . .
with cloyless sauce his appetite."

OYSTER SALAD.

One quart of oysters, boil up once, drain and cool. Cut in halves between the thick and thin parts; cover with vinegar and stand over night. Next day chop cabbage and celery, mix with oysters and pour over the following

DRESSING.

Yolks of 4 fresh, raw eggs and two hard boiled ones rubbed together until smooth. Add 4 tablespoonfuls oil, a few drops at a time, and mix well; then add two heaping teaspoonfuls salt, 1 of pepper, 1 of made mustard and 2 tablespoonfuls vinegar, added gradually.

MRS. F. CHAPMAN.

MACEDOINE SALAD.

One cup of chopped boiled beets, 1 cup of peas, 1 cup of string beans, ½ cup of asparagus tips, 10 drops of onion juice, 1 cup of chopped celery, mayonnaise dressing. MRS. E. M. DUNBAR.

"Use Imperial French Poultry Seasoning."

ENGLISH WALNUT SALAD.

One pint of English walnut meats, boiled until slightly softened, with 1 slice of onion, 1 bay-leaf and 1 teaspoonful of salt, drain and cool. Put a saltspoonful of salt and a dash of white pepper in a bowl; add a teaspoonful salad oil and 10 drops onion juice; rub until the salt is dissolved; add 2 tablespoonfuls of oil and 1 tablespoonful of vinegar; beat until whitish and thick. Serve on lettuce. Garnish with orange slices cut into 1/8 points. MRS. H. LOCKWOOD.

POTATO SALAD.

Boil and slice as many potatoes as are necessary. Salt them and stir in a few capers. Cut fine 1 small slice of onion and mix with the potatoes. Rub the yolks of 3 hard boiled eggs fine and mix with the yolk of one raw egg; add 1/4 teaspoonful of mustard, a pinch of red pepper, a little salt. Stir in oil until quite thick; add the whites, cut fine, and 3 tablespoonfuls of vinegar. MRS. G. D. COOK.

SPANISH SALAD.

Two cups of bits of bread, 2 cups of olives cut fine, 1 cup of chopped cucumber pickles; mayonaise dressing. SELECTED.

VALENTINES VARNISHES VALENTINE & COMPANY, Coach and Car Varnishes and Colors.

CUCUMBER SALAD.

Pare and cut in rather thick slices 50 fresh cucumbers of medium size. Put in a crock with 12 small onions, sliced, and 1 pint of salt. Let them stand all night. Strain and add 1 teacupful of white mustard seed, 1 of black, ¼ cup of celery seed and 1 cup of olive oil. Mix and cover with cold vinegar. Mrs. Rising.

FRENCH SALAD DRESSING.

A French salad dressing, made of 3 tablespoonfuls of olive oil, mixed well with ¼ teaspoonful of pepper, ½ teaspoonful of salt and when the mixture is well blended, add 1 tablespoonful of vinegar. If the salad dish is rubbed with a clove of garlic or a slice of onion, the dressing is improved. This is intended for simple salads of lettuce, cucumbers or string beans.

MARGUERITE SALAD.

Boil 6 eggs 20 minutes, rub yolks through sieve, and chop whites fine; moisten with boiled dressing or mayonnaise. Serve in cups of lettuce leaves, putting in each 1 teaspoonful of the yolks and around them the chopped whites.

POTATO PEPPER SALAD.

Put a layer of chopped cold potatoes in a dish and a

"Use Imperial French Poultry Seasoning."

layer of chopped green peppers, removing the seeds; pour over 1 tablespoonful of oil; fill the dish in this way and pour over it a mixture of ¼ cup of white vinegar, with 2 tablespoonfuls of water and ¼ teaspoonful of sugar.

POTATO SALAD.

Cut fine 6 cold boiled potatoes and 4 hard boiled eggs. Sprinkle over 1 teaspoonful of chopped parsley and one teaspoonful of onion juice, obtained by pressing a cut onion hard against a coarse grater. Serve with mayonnaise or cooked dressing.

MRS. E. M. DUNBAR.

TOMATO AND ONION SALAD.

Six firm, ripe tomatoes, peel and slice ¼ inch thick; slice very thin a Bermuda onion, arrange in layers in a salad bowl; pour over a dressing composed of 2 tablespoonfuls of salad oil, 2 tablespoonfuls of vinegar, ½ teaspoonful of salt, ½ teaspoonful of pepper. Use at once.

MRS. COCKRILL.

TURNIP SALAD.

Three sliced, cold, boiled turnips, 3 sliced beets, 1 sliced egg, hard boiled, 1 sliced onion; mayonnaise.

A salad may be made of grape fruit, oranges or lemons, by using the pulp only, serving it upon beds of

VALENTINES VARNISHES — **VALENTINE & COMPANY,** Coach and Car Varnishes and Colors.

lettuce, with a simple dressing of 3 tablespoonfuls of oil to 1 tablespoonful of vinegar, a little salt and pepper.

CELERY SALAD.

Grate a cocoanut and pour over it 1 pint of boiling water; let it stand until cool, squeeze the cocoanut dry, throwing it away. Strain the milky water and let it remain until a cream rises. Cut the tender white parts of celery quite fine and put in the salad bowl, scatter over it a tablespoonful of grated onion, a dash of cayenne and a little salt. Skim the cream from the cocoanut milk and pour it over the celery; add 1 tablespoonful of lemon juice. ·A FRIEND.

CABBAGE SALAD.

One-third head of cabbage, ⅓ Spanish onion, 3 stalks celery; chop fine; 3 eggs, well beaten, ½ teaspoonful of mustard, 1 tablespoonful of sugar, 2 tablespoonfuls of melted butter, small cup of vinegar; stir all together and cook until thick over boiling water and pour over salad while hot.

MRS. F. B. HOOKER.

VEGETABLE SALAD.

Equal quantities of celery, cabbage and pickled beets, cut fine; pour over them remoulade sauce, made by adding to the mashed ·yolks of 3 eggs, which have

---

"Use Imperial French Poultry Seasoning."

been boiled 20 minutes, ½ teaspoonful of made mustard; salt and pepper to taste; add ½ tablespoonful of tarragon vinegar and mix well; add, drop by drop, 3 tablespoonfuls of olive oil, stirring one way all the time; then, 1 raw yolk, and when well mixed, ½ tablespoonful of tarragon vinegar the last thing.

MRS. J. B. DANIELS.

COLD SLAW DRESSING.

Mix the yolks of 4 eggs, 1 teaspoonful of mustard, 2 tablespoonfuls of sugar, ½ cup of strong vinegar, weakened with three tablespoonfuls of water, a piece of butter the size of a walnut, and ½ teaspoonful of salt thoroughly together. Cook in double boiler until thick and pour over the cabbage when cold.

MRS. WALTER R. COMSTOCK.

SALAD DRESSING.

A FRENCH RECIPE.

Beat into the raw yolk of an egg enough oil to make the mixture as thick as cream. Cook 2 teaspoonfuls of corn starch in ½ cup of water, add 3 saltspoonfuls of salt, 1 of mustard, 1 of sugar and 3 tablespoonfuls of vinegar. Beat all together.   MISS FISHER.

VALENTINE & COMPANY,
Coach and Car Varnishes and Colors.

SALAD DRESSING.

One tablespoonful of flour, butter ½ the size of an egg, small teaspoonful of mustard, a little salt, a little red pepper, 1 teaspoonful sugar, ½ coffeecup of water, ½ coffeecup of vinegar. Cook thoroughly over boiling water, then beat the yolks of 3 eggs, stir in and cook a minute longer; then stand until thoroughly cold, when thin with cream. MRS. F. B. HOOKER.

SALAD DRESSING.

One-half pint of cream, 3 eggs, ½ cupful of vinegar, ⅓ cupful of butter, melted, 1 teaspoonful of salt, 1 level teaspoonful of sugar. Mustard and pepper may be added if desired. Boil in double boiler until it thickens, taking care it does not curdle. Bottle and keep cool.
MRS. J. B. WHEATLEY.

MAYONAISE DRESSING.

Yolk of 1 hard boiled egg, powdered, add 1 raw yolk, ½ teaspoonful each of salt and mustard, a little cayenne Stir this well and add by degrees salad oil, constantly beating. When nearly done, add vinegar or lemon juice, a small quantity. Set in a cool place.
MRS. W. D. McKEY.

SAUCE TARTARE.

One teaspoonful of mustard, 3 tablespoonfuls of

SALADS AND SAUCES.

vinegar, 1 tablespoonful of melted butter, 1 teaspoonful of salt, a dash of cayenne, 3 eggs beaten separately, whites added last. Cook until it thickens. When cold, add 1 cupful of whipped cream and some capers.

MRS. W. F. PARISH.

PARSLEY SAUCE.

One cupful of butter, 2 tablespoonfuls of chopped parsley, juice of 2 lemons, 1 tablespoonful of flour, cayenne and salt to taste. Boil a few minutes.

MRS. F. H. RADFORD.

WHITE SAUCE.

Into a frying pan put 3 tablespoonfuls of butter, 1 of chopped onion, 1 of chopped carrot, 2 of chopped celery, a bay leaf, a sprig of parsley and a sprig of thyme. Simmer slowly for ten minutes, being careful not to brown; then add 3 tablespoonfuls of flour, and stir until smooth and frothy. Draw the pan back to a cooler place and gradually add a pint of white stock. Stir until smooth, and add salt and pepper. Boil for five minutes and add ½ a cupful of cream or milk. Boil up once and after straining, use it. This is good for boiled fish or poultry, and is also a nice sauce in which to heat cold fish or meat.

MRS. H. P. KNAPP.

VALENTINES VARNISHES   **VALENTINE & COMPANY,**
Coach and Car Varnishes and Colors

TOMATO SAUCE.

Stew fresh or canned tomatoes until tender, then pass through a fine sieve. Return to saucepan, add 1 tablespoonful of flour and 1 of butter, rubbed together. Add ½ cup of stock or milk. Salt and pepper to taste. Simmer 25 minutes. Fine with veal cutlets.

MRS. A. E. TAYLOR.

SAUCE PIQUANTE.

Beat to a cream ½ cup of fresh butter; stir it over the fire until melted, adding finely chopped parsley and chives, and finishing with 1 tablespoonful of tarragon vinegar.

MRS. E. M. DUNBAR.

CARAMEL SAUCE.

One tea cup of brown sugar and ½ a cup of butter, put in a warm skillet and let it melt gradually, then boil until almost candy. Have ready 2 tablespoonfuls of flour, dissolved in a little cold water; pour a pint of boiling water over the candy, then add as much of the flour to make it the consistency you like. Flavor with vanilla.

MRS. W. H. FRENCH.

FOAMY SAUCE.

FOR STEAMED PUDDINGS.

Stir together ½ cup of butter, 1 cup of powdered sugar, 1 teaspoonful of vanilla, 2 tablespoonfuls of wine or fruit juice. Just before serving add ¼ cup of boiling

---

"Use Imperial French Poultry Seasoning."

water; stir well, then add the beaten white of 1 egg and beat until foamy.   MISS EDITH A. STEVENS.

PUDDING SAUCE.

One-third cup of butter, 1 cup of sugar, yolks of 4 eggs; cook until ropy, then add the whites of eggs, well beaten. Flavor with vanilla and serve hot. This is delicious with cottage pudding or any steamed pudding.
MRS. G. D. COOK.

SABYLLON MRS. HENDERSON.

Beat well 2 yolks and 1 whole egg with ½ teacup of sugar in a pan; set in boiling water; add ½ teacup of sherry wine, beating briskly until it thickens. Remove from the fire and add a little lemon juice.
MRS. J. P. MONTROSS.

SAUCE FOR BOILED TONGUE.

Brown 1 tablespoonful of butter, add 1 tablespoonful of flour and brown, add ½ pint of stock, stir until it boils; take from fire, add ½ teaspoonful of salt, a dash of pepper, 1 tablespoonful of mushroom catsup, 1 of tomato catsup. Bring to boiling point, pour over tongue and serve. *

VALENTINES VARNISHES **VALENTINE & COMPANY,** Coach and Car Varnishes and Colors.

FISH SAUCE.

One tablespoonful of butter, 1 teaspoonful of flour, rubbed together, 1 small grated onion, ½ pint of milk, salt and pepper to taste; 1 teaspoonful of horse radish. Boil 15 minutes. MRS. F. H. RADFORD.

SAUCE MAITRE d'HOTEL.

Stir in a saucepan over a slow fire a scant ½ pound of good butter, with salt and pepper and juice of ½ of a lemon, until the butter is nearly melted. Draw from the fire and stir until very smooth. Add the yolk of an egg and if not quite thick enough add a small teaspoonful of flour. Fine with chops or fish.

SALAD CREAM.

Heat 4 tablespoonfuls of butter and stir into it 1 tablespoonful of flour, being careful not to brown it. Add 1 cup of milk, stir until smooth and boil up once. Put the pan into hot water, beat 3 eggs with 1 teaspoonful of salt, 1 of dry mustard and a speck of cayenne pepper. Add ½ cup of vinegar and stir into the boiling milk until it thickens. Add 1 grated onion and 2 tablespoonfuls of minced parsley if this is used for potato salad. MRS. J. L. RHODES.

SWEETBREAD SALAD.

Select 2 large sweetbreads, let them lie in tepid water ½ hour, then boil in salted water 20 minutes, have water boiling before putting them in, than drop in cold water to harden; draw off the outer casing, remove the little pipes and cut into small dice. Cut into small pieces ½ pint of mushrooms and enough celery to equal both. Mix mayonnaise by putting the yolks of 3 eggs into a bowl, beat well and add a few drops of oil, stir until it disappears in the yolks, add a little more and so on, stirring until the last oil is blended into the yolks before adding more. When it is a pale opaque yellow "it has come" and oil can be added in larger quantities. In five minutes more it should be as thick as butter and cling to the spoon. Add a few drops of vinegar—this whitens it—stir a few seconds and it will look like cream, and then add oil until it is very thick again. Then add a dessertspoonful of vinegar, a saltspoonful of salt and a little white pepper; if liked a sprinkle of cayenne. Pour over the above mixture, reserving a little for the top. Toss and mix thoroughly. Spread the remainder over the top and garnish with white celery tips and olives

F. S. M.

OYSTER SALAD.

Two dozen fresh oysters, 2 heads of celery, with part of their green tops, about ½ as much tender, white cabbage, mayonnaise salad dressing. After washing the celery and cabbage throw them into boiling salted water, let boil 5 minutes, then drain and chop them fine. The green cel-

ery leaves will acquire an intenser green in the boiling water and add to the appearance of the salad. Drain the liquor from the oysters and boil and skim it. Add an equal quantity of vinegar, some broken peppercorns, pepper sauce and salt. Put in the oysters and keep shaking the pan while they are scalding, that they may set in round and plump shape. Do not let them boil. Drain and set them away in a dish to become ice cold. When to be served season the chopped celery and cabbage slightly with oil and vinegar. Spread part of it in a dish or in individual dishes, place the oysters in it side by side and the rest of the celery on top of them. Smooth the top a little and pour mayonnaise over just thin enough to run.

Mrs. Crawford.

OLIVE SAUCE.

Place 2 dozen olives in an earthen bowl. Pour over them enough hot water to cover and let remain ½ hour to draw out the brine. Place 2 tablespoonfuls of butter in the frying-pan. When it commences to color add one tablespoonful of flour; stir until smooth, and after it has cooked for 2 minutes add 1 pint of stock and place in a gentle heat to simmer. Pare the olives round and round, the same as paring an apple, leaving the pulp in a single strip. If this is done carefully the olives will retain their shape. Place the olives in the sauce; add a dash of salt and pepper and a teaspoonful of lemon juice. Simmer 20 minutes. Skim carefully and serve.

"Use Imperial French Poultry Seasoning."

SALADS AND SAUCES.

CELERY AND NUT SALAD.

One cup each of chopped celery and English walnuts, a little salt, ½ cup of mayonnaise dressing, to which has been added 1 cup of sweet cream. Serve in a bed of blanched celery leaves. D. M. E.

OYSTER SAUCE.

Two tablespoonfuls of butter in a saucepan, 1 teaspoonful of minced onions and parsley; fry lightly; add 1 cup of oyster liquor, 1 cup of oyster meats and the yolks of 2 eggs, a little salt and pepper; stir till thick, but do not let boil.

WALNUT FISH SAUCE.

Work into a cup of nice butter as much lemon juice as it will take. When creamy add ½ teacupful of chopped pickled walnuts or pickled cucumbers with a little minced parsley.

APRICOT AND FIG SAUCE.

Cook until soft a pint of dried apricots; scald and chop ½ dozen layer figs and add them to the apricots. Let them cook together 15 minutes, adding a cup of white sugar. The combination is very pleasant.

SAUCE A LA GENOESE.

Melt slowly 3 ounces of butter, juice of a lemon, well beaten yolks of 2 eggs, grated rind of ½ lemon, salt and

VALENTINE VARNISHES   VALENTINE & COMPANY, Coach and Car Varnishes and Colors

pepper, a suspicion of garlic. Stir until thick and use at once. This is for cutlets, steaks, etc.

Mrs. J. E. Brown.

RASPBERRY OR STRAWBERRY SAUCE.

Boil a large cup of fresh berries, ½ pint of water, 2 tablespoonfuls of sugar, strained juice of ½ lemon, until soft, rub through a sieve, add a tablespoonful of brandy and serve. In winter, jam can be used and sherry instead of brandy.

Mrs. Crawfod.

FRUIT JUICE FOR PUDDING SAUCE AND JELLIES.

Four pounds of red raspberries, 1½ ounces of cream of tartar, 1½ quarts of cold water, 2¼ pounds of sugar, to 1 quart of juice. Mash berries and cream of tartar together, add the water and let stand 24 hours. Strain, and add 2¼ pounds of sugar to every quart of juice. Let it remain on the stove until it just comes to a boil, then take off. When cold put into bottles. Tie a muslin cloth over the bottle. Do not seal.

Mrs. C. W. Crary.

BREAKFAST.

"Dinner may be pleasant,
So may social tea
But yet, methinks the breakfast
Is best of all the three"—Anon.

RICE MUFFINS.

One cup of milk, 1½ cups of flour, ½ cup of cold boiled rice, 2 scant teaspoonfuls of Cameo baking powder, a pinch of salt, a teaspoonful of sugar, a heaping teaspoonful of butter and 1 egg. Mix the dry ingredients and rub them through a sieve into a bowl. Melt the butter and beat it into the rice. Beat the egg and add it to the milk. Add this mixture to the dry ingredients, then stir in the rice, beating all together quickly and well. Bake in gem pans 25 minutes in a moderate oven.   MRS. E. JONES

BREAKFAST PUFFS.

Sift together ½ pint of flour, pinch of salt, 2 tablespoonfuls of Cameo baking powder. Stir into this gradually a gill of milk. Add the yolks of two eggs, then the whites whipped to a foam. Pour into gem pans and bake in a quick oven.

VALENTINES VARNISHES   **VALENTINE & COMPANY,**
Coach and Car Varnishes and Colors.

RICE PANCAKES.

One pint of soft boiled rice; stir in 2 tablespoonfuls of butter while rice is hot, and let cool; and ½ cup of milk, ½ cup of flour and 2 eggs well beaten; bake at once on hot griddle. Miss Emily White.

BENJAMIN.

For this dish a round thick cracker must be used. Split, toast, butter each half and put into a deep, hot dish. Heat to boiling point enough rich milk to cover your crackers; melt in this a scant teaspoonful of butter, salt to taste, and thicken very little. Just before serving pour this over the crackers, cover closely and do not let it wait a minute before being eaten.

RAISED HOMINY WAFFLES.

The small hominy is best for these. To a coffee cup of boiled hominy add 1 pint of boiled milk and 1 tablespoonful of butter, 1 pint of flour, 1 teaspoonful of salt, 1 tablespoonful of sugar and a scant half-teacup of yeast. Beat well, cover, set in a warm place over night. In the morning add 2 well-beaten eggs, yokes and whites separately. Bake in waffle irons. This recipe answers as well for muffins if it is not convenient to made waffles.

Contributed.

"Use Imperial French Poultry Seasoning."

BREAKFAST.

FRIED HOMINY CAKES.

One large cup of cooked coarse hominy, 1 tablespoonful of flour, 1 egg or 2 yolks. Take cold hominy that has been well cooked and is dry and pound with a potato masher to make it adhesive; mix in egg and flour. Make it out in flat biscuit-shaped cakes with floured hands and fry brown in a frying pan.

BREAKFAST BUNS.

Two cups of flour, ¾ cup of corn meal, ¾ cup of shortening, ½ cup of sugar, 2 eggs, 1 cup of sweet milk, 2 teaspoonfuls of Cameo baking powder. Bake 20 minutes in hot gem pans. Cottolene will shorten these buns as nicely as butter, but remember to use only half the given quantity.

SOUTHERN SLAPPERS.

Stir a quart of southern meal into a bowl; add a teaspoonful of salt and 1 of sugar; pour in boiling water, stirring as you pour, till the meal is well moistened, but not thinned. Let stand a few minutes to swell, then add cold sweet milk sufficient to make a rather thin batter, break 2 eggs into the batter, beating briskly with the spoon. Fry upon a hot, well-greased griddle. M. W.

WAFFLES.

Mix 1 pint of sifted flour with ⅔ of a pint of milk until a smooth paste; beat in a tablespoonful of melted butter

VALENTINES VARNISHES — VALENTINE & COMPANY, Coach and Car Varnishes and Colors.

and a little salt, and lastly 2 eggs beaten light. Have waffle iron hot and ready greased, pour in enough batter to cover the lower side and close the upper one gently down upon it. Keep over fire half a minute and turn over for same length of time. Remove and place in oven a few moments to crisp.

CORN MEAL SLAP JACKS.

Scald over night 2 cups of Indian meal with a quart of boiling milk or milk and water mixed, adding 1 tablespoonful of butter, 1 tablespoonful of brown sugar or molasses. Cover closely and let it stand until morning, when add yolks of 2 well-beaten eggs, 1 scant cup of flour and 1 teaspoonful of salt. Heat and grease the griddle, and then add to the batter 1 teaspoonful of soda dissolved in a little hot milk; and, last of all, whites of 2 eggs beaten stiff, stirred in lightly. If the batter is too stiff in the morning, stir in a little cold milk. L. A.

LAPLANDERS.

One pint of milk, 1 pint of flour, 2 eggs, small teaspoonful of salt. Mix the salt with the flour, add part of the milk slowly until a smooth paste is formed. Add a piece of butter—melted—the size of the bowl of a tablespoon and the remainder of the milk with the beaten yolks, and, lastly, the whites beaten to a stiff froth. Cook in well-buttered gem pans in a quick oven until they are brown

---

"Use Imperial French Poultry Seasoning."

GRIDDLE ROLLS.

and well popped over, which will be in about 20 minutes.

Prepare an ordinary wheat-cake batter; have the gridiron hot; bake each cake the size of a lunch plate. Soon as each cake is done, quickly spread with butter and cover with maple sugar, roll into a neat roll, lay in a covered dish, placed over boiling water till all are done, and then serve. A VERMONT FRIEND.

FLANNEL CAKES.

Sift together 1½ pints of flour, 1 tablespoonful of brown sugar, 2 tablespoonfuls of Cameo baking powder, and 1 teaspoonful of salt. Add 2 beaten eggs and 1½ pints of milk and beat into a smooth, thin batter, adding a tablespoonful of melted butter. Bake on hot griddle to a rich brown color and serve with maple syrup. These should never be larger than a tea saucer.

WORLD'S FAIR.

RICE CAKES.

Two cups of boiled rice, 2 eggs, a pinch of salt, 1 teaspoonful of sugar, 1 of butter, beat all well together. Add 1 teaspoonful of Cameo baking powder, a cup of milk and flour enough to thicken so that the cakes will turn easily. Drop by spoonfuls into a frying pan half full of hot lard, and fry light brown.

VALENTINES VARNISHES **VALENTINE & COMPANY,** Coach and Car Varnishes and Colors.

BREAKFAST.

GRAHAM PUFFS.

Two cups of Graham flour, 1 tablespoonful of melted butter, 2 eggs, 1 quart of milk, ½ teaspooonful of salt, 1 teaspoonful of Cameo baking powder. Sift together the flour and baking powder; add butter and salt to the milk and drop in the eggs, without beating. Beat into this the prepared flour, making a smooth paste as stiff as for griddle cakes. Drop into hot and well greased gem pans and bake at once in a hot oven.

SYRUP FOR WAFFLES.

Boil 2 cups of sugar and a little water until it is a thick, rich syrup; about 5 minutes. Add 1 tablespoonful of butter and allow it to melt, then remove from the fire and stir in 2 tablespoonfuls of cinnamon. Serve immediately.
Mrs. J. R. Flood.

CORN BREAD.

Put 1 quart of milk on the fire, in a double boiler; when it comes to a boil stir in 4 large kitchen spoonfuls of cornmeal and cook 5 minutes—stirring all the time. Remove from the fire and stir once or twice as it cools. When cool add 3 eggs well beaten with 2 tablespoonfuls flour, 1 tablespoonful butter, 1 pinch salt. Pour in a greased dish and bake 35 minutes. Serve immediately with napkin around dish.

"Use Imperial French Poultry Seasoning."

GRAHAM BISCUITS.

One pint of graham flour and ½ pint of wheat flour, 1 tablespoonful of lard or butter, 1 teaspoonful of sugar, 1 saltspoonful of salt, 2 teaspoonfuls of Cameo baking powder, sifted in with the wheat flour (do not sift brown flour); mix with enough very cold water to make a smooth paste to roll on the board; roll out ½ an inch thick, cut and bake in very hot oven.

FOAM GRIDDLE CAKES.

One-half pint of sour milk, pinch of salt, yolk of 1 egg, a piece of butter size of a hickory nut, enough flour to make a batter; beat all together for 5 minutes, then add ⅓ of a teaspoonful of soda dissolved in 1 tablespoonful of boiling water, and lastly the white of the egg, beaten to a stiff froth and stirred in slowly and carefully as for sponge cake. Bake immediately on a hot griddle. The nicest way to grease a griddle is to use a large piece of beef suet tied in a thin cloth. Mrs. F. H. Wait.

CORN MUFFINS.

One cup yellow cornmeal, ½ cup of flour, 1 large tablespoonful of sugar, 1½ teaspoonfuls Cameo baking powder, 1 beaten egg, 1½ cups of sweet milk, a saltspoonful salt; bake in hot greased gem pans.

VALENTINE & COMPANY, Coach and Car Varnishes and Colors.

HOT ROLLS.

Pare, boil and mash 2 white potatoes with 2 spoonfuls of lard; stir in a cupful of scalded milk, with ¼ of yeast cake, dissolved in the milk after it cools; a teaspoonful of salt, 2 of sugar, 1 egg, beaten light, flour enough to make a firm dough; set to rise over night; in the morning work and roll out on your bread board to an inch thick, cut with a biscuit-cutter, put in your pan an inch apart, set to raise for ½ an hour, bake in a quick oven.   MRS. H. M. D.

RAISED FLANNEL CAKES.

Boil a pint and a half of sweet milk and let it stand till lukewarm. Add 2 large tablespoonfuls yeast and pour upon 1 pint flour, ½ pint cornmeal, 1 teaspoonful salt and 1 tablespoonful sugar, mixed well together. Cover closely and put in a warm place. In the morning add 2 eggs, beaten separately. Let the batter stand 15 minutes, if convenient, after adding the eggs. Bake on a hot griddle.

DROPPED BISCUIT.

With a pint of flour sift 2 teaspoonfuls of sugar, ½ a teaspoonful of salt and 1½ teaspoonfuls of Cameo baking powder; rub in a dessertspoonful of butter or lard and add milk till too stiff for stirring but still too soft for kneading, and drop in small mounds on a buttered tin. Leave some space between the biscuits and bake 10 or 12 minutes in a quick oven.   F. G. S.

"Use Imperial French Poultry Seasoning."

FLAPJACKS.

Make a batter of 1 pint of sour milk, 1 even teaspoonful of baking soda and a little salt, with wheat flour enough to thicken sufficiently to fry nicely. Fry in cakes the size of an ordinary breakfast plate. Butter each cake and sprinkle it with sugar, piling them one on top of another. A little grated nutmeg improves them. Have the batter as thin as it is possible to turn the cakes well. These are delicious, especially if sour cream is used.

SALLY LUNN.

Set to rise over night a stiff batter made of a pint of new milk warmed, 1 tablespoonful butter, 1 tablespoonful sugar, a little salt, 1 teacup yeast, 2 well beaten eggs and flour to stiffen. Put in a warm place. In the morning add flour to knead, and work it until smooth—about 15 minutes. About 2 hours before luncheon roll to a ½ inch thickness and cut the size of a round jelly-cake tin. Put into a greased tin, rub over with melted butter, and lay upon it another round, likewise rubbed with butter. When light bake in a moderate oven; raise the upper part just before sending to table and butter between the layers. Cut in triangles as you would a pie. C. W. A.

VALENTINES VARNISHES VALENTINE & COMPANY, Coach and Car Varnishes and Colors.

MUFFINS.

One tablespoonful of soft butter, 2 tablespoonfuls of sugar; rub to a cream; 2 beaten eggs, a saltspoonful of salt, 1 cup of sweet milk, 2 rounding teaspoonfuls of Cameo baking powder, 2 cups of flour. Bake in buttered muffin rings.

HOMINY GRIDDLE CAKES.

To 1 pint of warm boiled hominy add 1 pint of sour milk and 1 pint of flour. Beat 2 eggs and stir into the batter, a pinch of salt and soda enongh to cover point of teaspoon.

HOT BISCUIT.

Rub into 1 quart of flour 2 tablespoonfuls of butter and lard, equal parts; add 1 tablespoonful of white sugar, ½ teaspoonful of salt and 2 heaping teaspoonfuls of Cameo baking powder. Put all these things through a sieve 3 times; then with a wooden spoon stir lightly in sufficient milk or milk and water to make a thick batter, or rather a thin dough; turn out upon a well floured molding board, flatten lightly with the bowl of the spoon until about an inch thick and cut out with a very small-sized cooky cutter; lightly place in a greased baking-tin, barely touching each other, and bake in a hot oven. Delicious and digestible if quickly and lightly handled. Mrs. G. W. N.

"Use Imperial French Poultry Seasoning."

LUNCH ROLLS.

Sift together 1 pint of flour, 1 teaspoonful of Cameo baking powder and ½ a tablespoonful of salt; work in 1 teaspoonful of lard and add ½ pint of milk; mix to a smooth dough; roll out to ½ inch thickness, cut into circular shapes and bake in moderate oven.

SQUASH GRIDDLE CAKES.

One cup boiling milk, 1 cup sifted squash, 1 tablespoonful of butter, 1 tablespoonful of sugar, ½ teaspoonful of salt, 1 egg, 2 teaspoonfuls of Cameo baking powder and 1 cup of flour. Pour the boiling milk into the squash; add the butter, sugar and salt. When cool add the egg, well beaten, then the baking powder mixed with the flour. Fry a delicate brown.

SINGING HINNEY.

Take 1 quart of flour and sift 2 teaspoonfuls of Cameo baking powder into it; rub in 1 tablespoonful of lard; add 1 teaspoonful of salt and 1 well-beaten egg. Moisten with just enough sweet milk to make into dough, not too stiff; roll out and bake on greased griddle; when it is cooked on one side turn it over and let it cook till a pale brown on the other side; then split it open, butter it and put together again; cut it into 3 cornered pieces and serve it hot.

VALENTINES VARNISHES **VALENTINE & COMPANY,** Coach and Car Varnishes and Colors.

BREAKFAST.

PANCAKES.

Soak 2 or 3 slices of dried bread in a pint of sour milk over night; in the morning add a small half teaspoonful of baking soda and salt, one egg, flour enough to make a thin batter. Serve with syrup.

HOMINY MUFFINS.

Hash 1 cup of boiled hominy fine with a fork, add 1 cup of corn meal, half a cup of milk, 2 teaspoonfuls melted butter, 2 teaspoonfuls sugar, 1 egg, 1 teaspoonful Cameo baking powder. Beat thoroughly and hard. Put into gem pans and bake fifteen minutes.   A. R.

CORN MUFFINS.

Beat 2 eggs very light, add 1 teaspoonful of melted butter, 1 tablespoonful of brown sugar, 2 teacupfuls corn meal, 1 heaping tablespoonful of flour, to which add 1 teaspoonful of Cameo baking powder and a cupful of milk. Mix thoroughly, pour into greased muffin tins and bake in a quick oven.

FLANNEL CAKES.

One egg, well beaten, butter size of a walnut, ½ pint of sour milk, ½ teaspoonful of soda, 3 tablespoonfuls of flour, 1 tablespoonful of corn meal, a little salt.
    M. F. REEVES

"Use Imperial French Poultry Seasoning."

BREAKFAST.

RICE WAFFLES.

To a pint of soft-boiled rice add 1 teaspoonful salt and a pint of flour, into which 2 teaspoonfuls of Cameo baking powder has been sifted. Beat the whites and yolks of 2 eggs separately; add to the yolks a large cup sweet milk and pour into the rice with a teaspoonful melted butter. Add the beaten whites last. Beat gently until smooth and bake without delay.

SPANISH BUNS.

Two eggs, 2 cups brown sugar, ¾ of a cup of butter, 1 cup of milk, 2 teaspoonfuls of Cameo baking powder, 2 teaspoonfuls ground cinnamon, 2 teaspoonfuls ground cloves, 2½ cups of sifted flour. Cream the butter and sugar, add the eggs, well beaten, then the milk, and lastly stir in the flour, sifted with the cinnamon, cloves and baking powder. Form into small rolls and bake in moderate oven twenty minutes. For frosting use the whites of 2 eggs, 1 teaspoonful of cinnamon, 1 of cloves and thicken with brown sugar.   MOTHER'S.

BREAKFAST SHORTCAKE.

Sift and mix thoroughly a scant quart of flour, 2 heaped teaspoonfuls Cameo baking powder, 1 teaspoonful of salt, 1 teaspoonful sugar; rub into this 1 tablespoonful each of lard and butter and add sweet milk enough to form

---

VALENTINES VARNISHES **VALENTINE & COMPANY,** Coach and Car Varnishes and Colors

a dough just stiff enough to roll out; roll rather less than half an inch thick and bake in light layer cake pans; have ready 2 teacups of finely chopped meat and ½ teacup chopped or mashed cold potato; heat this on a skillet, with a large tablespoonful of butter, a half teacup water, a cup milk, a quarter teaspeonful salt, a good pinch of pepper; thicken this with a teaspoonful each of flour and butter rubbed together; split the cakes, butter them and spread the creamed meat between; there will be three thin layers, and if liked one can be reserved to have a layer of berries, peaches, prunes or other fruit between and sprinkled with sugar while hot. D.

FRIED CORNMEAL MUFFINS.

Mix 1 pint sifted Indian meal with 1 teaspoonful salt and 1 tablespoonful sugar; pour gradually on this 1 pint boiling water; cover after beating well and set away until morning; add 2 well beaten eggs; beat thoroughly; dip a tablespoon in cold milk and with the wet spoon dip up the batter by the tablespoonful and fry in boiling lard; turn each one while cooking. SELECTED.

GRAHAM GEMS.

One and one-half cups graham flour, 1 cup wheat flour, 1 tablespoonful butter, 1 teaspoonful sugar, 2

"Use Imperial French Poultry Seasoning."

large teaspoonfuls Cameo baking powder, 2 eggs, 1 teaspoonful salt, 2 cups milk. Bake twelve minutes.
MRS. WILLIAM L. SHIDE.

DIXIE BISCUIT.

Three pints flour, 2 eggs, 2 tablespoonfuls lard, 1 cup milk, yeast. Mix at 11 o'clock a. m. Roll out at 4 o'clock and cut with 2 sizes of cutters, putting the smaller one on top; let it rise until time to get dinner and bake 20 minutes. MRS. BEN WILLIAMS.

JOHNNY CAKE.

One cup corn meal, 1 of flour, 1 of sweet milk, ½ of butter, ½ of sugar, 2 eggs, a little salt, 2 teaspoonfuls Cameo baking powder. MRS. F. B. HOOKER.

HOT CORN BREAD.

One pint sour or buttermilk, ⅔ cup sugar, 2 of corn meal, 1 of flour, 1 egg, 1 teaspoonful soda, ½ of salt, butter size of an egg. MRS. B. R. WELLS.

SOUR CREAM BISCUIT.

One large cup sour milk, ½ cup sour cream, 1 teaspoonful soda, a little salt, flour enough to mix soft.
MRS. ARTHUR SMITH.

VALENTINE & COMPANY,
Coach and Car Varnishes and Colors.

BREAKFAST.

ROLLS.

One pint scalded milk, ½ cup butter, 1 tablespoonful sugar, ½ yeast cake, dissolved in warm water; 2 whites of eggs beaten well. Rub butter and sugar to a cream, add egg, milk, then flour. MRS. A. G. JONES.

BALTIMORE BISCUIT.

To 1 quart flour add 1 teaspoonful salt and a tablespoonful lard, with water enough to moisten to a stiff dough. This must be worked or pounded an hour. Roll by hand into round balls, flatten slightly and prick with a fork. MRS. GEO. L. PADDOCK.

POTATO ROLLS.

Two cups boiled potato, pressed through a colander, 2 eggs, ½ cup lard, 1 cup yeast, 2 tablespoonfuls sugar, a little salt. Mix this in the morning; when light, add flour enough to make into dough and let it rise again. Roll out and cut into cakes, place in a pan, not too close together. Let it rise again and bake 8 or 10 minutes. MRS. J. F. DICKSON.

RICE BISCUIT.

Stir 2 eggs into 1 pint boiled rice while warm, make

"Use Imperial French Poultry Seasoning."

into small biscuit with the hands, roll in flour, bake on buttered tins in a quick oven. Eat hot with butter.

Mrs. F. H. Radford.

CORN MEAL MUFFINS.

One cup boiled rice, 1 of flour, ½ of milk, 2 eggs, 2 tablespoonfuls corn meal, 1 of melted butter, 1 (heaping) of sugar, 2 of Cameo baking powder, 1 of salt.

Mrs. J. Y. Scammon.

RICE MUFFINS.

One cup milk, 1 of boiled rice, 2 teaspoonfuls Cameo baking powder, 1 tablespoonful sugar, a scant pint of flour.

Mrs. L. B. Turrill.

RICE MUFFINS—NO. 2.

Beat hard 1 cup cold boiled rice, 2 eggs, 1 pint flour, 1 tablespoonful lard or butter, 1 teaspoonful salt, enough milk to make a thin batter. Bake in quick oven.

Mrs. M. L. Bradley.

WAFFLES.

One pint sweet milk, 3 eggs well beaten, 1 tablespoonful melted butter, 2 teaspoonfuls Cameo baking powder, salt, flour enough to make a thin batter. Bake in hot waffle irons, which should never be greased.

Mrs. Arthur Smith.

VALENTINES VARNISHES **VALENTINE & COMPANY,**
Coach and Car Varnishes and Colors.

VIENNA PUFFS.

Crumble ½ yeast cake into 1 cup warm water, add ½ teacup sugar and set it in a warm place until it rises to the surface, add to it 1 pint flour, one tablespoonful butter, ½ teaspoonful salt, 1 tablespoonful sugar and 1 egg; mix all well together, cover and let it rise until morning; butter gem pans, fill half full and bake quickly.

A. F. S.

TEA BREAD.

Beat a piece of butter the size of an egg to a cream with ¼ cup sugar and add the yolks of 2 eggs well beaten. Beat vigorously and add 2 cups milk. Sift 4 cups flour with 2½ teaspoonfuls Cameo baking powder. Pour the above mixture into the flour until smooth and beat the batter until it blisters; then fold in the beaten whites of the eggs and bake 20 minutes in 2 pans.

M. E. D.

NEWPORT LOAF.

Cream together a half cup each of butter and sugar, add the yolks of two eggs and 1 cup sweet milk, add 1½ pints sifted flour, with 2 teaspoonfuls Cameo baking powder. Stir in lightly the beaten whites of 2 eggs.

"Use Imperial French Poultry Seasoning."

CORN BREAD.

Cream ¾ cup sugar and ½ cup of butter, add 3 well-beaten eggs, a little salt and 1 pint sweet milk. Mix together 2 cups flour and 1 scant cup corn meal; sift this with 3 teaspoonfuls Cameo baking powder and add it to the first mixture. Butter muffin pans and fill half full. Bake in quick oven. M. H. W.

POTATO BISCUIT.

Heat 1 cup of milk and 2 cups of water, add 2 tablespoonfuls of butter, 1 tablespoonful of sugar and 1 tablespoonful of salt. When just warm add 1 pint of mashed potato, into which one egg has been stirred, flour to make a stiff dough, add 3 tablespoonfuls of yeast, or ½ compressed yeast cake. Let rise, make into biscuit, and raise again. bake in a moderate oven. Mrs. W. H. H. Peirce.

VALENTINES VARNISHES **VALENTINE & COMPANY,**
Coach and Car Varnishes and Colors.

LUNCHEON.

*Some hae meat that canna eat,
And some would eat that want it;
But we hae meat and we can eat,
Sae let the Lord be thankit—Burns.*

SALPICON.

Brown lightly 1 tablespoonful of butter and 1 of flour, add 1 cup of stock and a glass of white wine, also a bouquet of herbs, salt and pepper, cook a few minutes and add equal portions of any cold meats, game, ham, tongue, cook over a slow fire, remove the herbs, thicken with a little flour, serve in vol-au-vents or pates.

Mrs. F. H. Wait.

ENTREMET.

Put into a dish 1½ cups of cold mashed turnip, 1½ of mashed potatoes, 1 cup of cream, 1 tablespoonful of melted butter, beaten yolks of 2 eggs, salt and pepper. Strew crumbs over the top with bits of butter and bake 20 minutes.

"Use Imperial French Poultry Seasoning."

MEXICAN POTATOES.

Pare and halve large potatoes, scoop out the center and fill with a mixture made as follows: boil 2 eggs 20 minutes and mash the yolks fine, chopping the whites very fine. Mix with them finely chopped meat, 1 raw egg, beaten, 1 tablespoonful of minced parsley, 1 of grated onion, and one of melted butter. Heap the mixture in the potatoes and sprinkle over the top crumbs and grated cheese. Bake to a brown and pour tomato sauce around them.

STUFFED ROLLS.

Cut off the end of a roll and remove the inside. Fill with a mixture of cheese, minced ham or chicken, covering the top with the small piece cut off.

MOCK HARE.

Mix 1 pound of sausage meat with ½ pound of fine chopped beef, soak 3 slices of bread in cold water until soft, press out all the water, place 1 tablespoonful of butter and 1 chopped onion in a pan, stir and cook without browning 5 minutes, remove and when cold, add it to the meat; add 1 egg, pepper and salt to taste, form into a long, round loaf, brush it over with water, place

VALENTINES VARNISHES VALENTINE & COMPANY,
Coach and Car Varnishes and Colors.

3 slices of thin pork in a pan, lay the loaf upon it, put 3 slices on the roll, bake about ½ an hour. Baste with stock or gravy.

VEAL PIE.

Two pounds of veal, not too fat. Remove the bone and put it with the fat and refuse bits such as gristle and skin, in a saucepan, with a large teacup of cold water to make gravy. Cut the veal into thin, even slices and lay it in the bottom of a pudding dish, cover with a layer of hard-boiled eggs, sliced, buttered and peppered; next, a layer of very thin strips of salt pork or ham upon which a few drops of lemon juice have been squeezed. Continue until the dish is full. Line the sides with good pie-crust and pour over the gravy, which should be seasoned with pepper, salt and herbs, and strained. Cover with crust and bake 2 hours. Mrs. F. H. Wait.

PHILADELPHIA SCRAPPLE.

Four pounds of lean, raw pork, from the shoulder, 1¼ pounds of calf's liver, ½ pound of leaf lard. Put in cold water and boil until tender. Chop fine, add 2 large tablespoonfuls of salt, pepper to taste, both red and black, season with sage or sweet marjoram, return

---

"Use Imperial French Poultry Seasoning."

LUNCHEON.

to kettle and thicken with equal parts of buckwheat flour and corn meal. Rinse the pan with cold water, pour in the mixture and when cold, slice and fry.

Miss. M. L. Byllesby.

CHICKEN CROQUETTES.

Boil 2 chickens, with 1 carrot, 1 onion, and 6 whole cloves; chop fine. Rub 2 tablespoonfuls of flour into 1 of butter and stir it into a cup of the chicken broth, which must be boiling; add the chopped meat with a dash of nutmeg. Put it aside to cool. When cold, shape, dip in beaten egg and throw grated bread crumbs at them until covered. Chopped mushrooms improve them. Fry light brown. Mrs. J. M. Taylor.

CHICKEN CROQUETTES.—No. 2.

Chop fine 2 sweet breads and 2 pounds of chicken. Melt 2 tablespoonfuls of butter and stir into it 1 tablespoonful of flour, add by degrees 1 gill of cream, stir until it boils, add 1 dessertspoonful of minced parsley, ¼ teaspoonful of grated onion, pepper and salt to taste. Take from the fire and add the meat, stir well and cool. When cold and firm form into oval shape, dip in beaten white of egg, roll in cracker dust. Set aside for an hour, then place in frying basket and brown.

Mrs. R. S. Thompson.

LUNCHEON.

CURRIED EGGS.

Boil 1 quart of peas in salted water 10 minutes press through a colander free from water, return to pan, add 1 tablespoonful of butter, 1 of stock, ½ teaspoonful of salt and keep hot. Cut 6 hard boiled eggs in slices and lay in center of hot dish. Put 1 gill of cream in pan, add 1 teaspoonful of onion juice and 1 of curry powder, stir until it boils, pour it over the eggs, put the puree around and serve.   Mrs. J. P. Montross.

SCALLOPED CHICKEN.

Cut up a large chicken and stew gently until tender, then remove the bones, cutting the meat small. Return to saucepan, adding stock seasoned with pepper and salt. Put in 1 pint of small mushrooms, simmer 15 minutes, thicken with flour, put into baking dish, cover with cracker crumbs, wet with melted butter, brown in the oven and serve hot with boiled rice and currant jelly. This serves six persons.   Mrs. James Hewitt.

CAPE MAY CLAM FRITTERS.

Four tablespoonfuls of sifted flour, 1½ teaspoonfuls of Cameo baking powder, 1 egg, ½ cup of milk, 2 dozen clams chopped very fine. Fry in plenty of boiling lard.
                    Mrs. R. S. Thompson.

A. N. Warner & Co.   DRY GOODS,
53rd St. & Lake Ave., Chicago

PILAF.

One pound of Hamburg steak fried and separated while frying, so it is like hash. Season. One-half can of tomatoes stewed and seasoned, 1 cup of boiled rice. Stir all together thoroughly, turn into baking dish, cover and bake nearly 2 hours. Serve hot, or mold and slice when cold. If preferred, maccaroni may be used instead of rice. MRS. H. L. HUMPHREY.

PARSNIP NUTS.

Boil the parsnips and mash fine. To 1 pint add 1 teaspoonful of salt, 2 tablespoonfuls of melted butter, a dash of pepper and 2 tablespoonfuls of milk. Mix well over the fire and when very hot add a well beaten egg and spread out to cool. Take the meat of an English walnut and envelop it in the parsnip pulp. Roll in egg and crumbs and fry light brown. SELECTED.

VITELLA.

Melt 1 tablespoonful of butter in a saucepan but do not brown it, add 1 tablespoonful of flour and stir until smooth, season with salt and pepper and gradually mix with it ½ pint of stock or boiling water. When it thickens and is quite smooth add 1 cup of veal cut in small, thin slices. Just before serving stir in the beaten yolk of an egg and do not let it boil again; serve immediately. SELECTED.

VALENTINES VARNISHES VALENTINE & COMPANY, Coach and Car Varnishes and Colors.

A DELICIOUS DISH.

Cut the tops from 6 large tomatoes and remove the inside pulp. Mix 2 tablespoonfuls of bread crumbs, 1 of chopped parsley, ¼ pound of finely minced ham, ½ tablespoonful of butter, the juice of ½ a lemon, cayenne and salt to taste; add the white of an egg, well beaten, and the pulp from the tomatoes. Stuff the tomatoes with this mixture, replace the tops and lay them in a well buttered dish, bake a ½ hour, lay each one on a slice of toast, well buttered, garnish with parsley and serve hot. MRS. BEN. WILLIAMS.

SPAGHETTI ITALIENNE.

Procure the yellow spaghetti which comes in coils. Put it in a colander set in hot salted water and boil ½ hour. Allow one heaping tablespoonful of grated Edam cheese to each plate. Make a sauce of 1 quart can of tomatoes, 1 small chopped onion, a dozen cloves. Boil until thick. Put it through a sieve, return to the fire, add butter, salt, a little cayenne pepper, a dash of Worcestershire sauce and a few chopped mushrooms. In serving, first put spaghetti on the plate, then a small butter ball, a heaping tablespoonful of the cheese and 2 of the sauce. The spaghetti and sauce should be *hot*.

MRS. HARRY L. ASHTON.

A. N. Warner & Co. BUTTRICK PATTERNS, 53rd St. & Lake Ave., Chicago

MACCARONI WITH SAUCE A LA MILANESE.

Melt 2 tablespoonfuls of butter, add 4 cloves of garlic, brown well and skim out, add 10 tablespoonfuls of cooked tomatoes and simmer down ½. Have ready boiled maccaroni about 1 cupful, stir it into the sauce with a few shredded olives and pour it all over fried veal cutlets.
Mrs. F. H. Wait.

SALMON LOAF.

One large can of salmon, 1 cup of bread crumbs, 4 eggs, 3 tablespoonfuls of butter, pepper and salt. Steam 1½ hours and serve with tomato sauce.
Miss Helen M. Topping.

FRICANDELLE.

Chop fine ½ pound each of veal, fresh pork and beef, add 3 eggs well beaten, 2 cups of moist bread crumbs, a small minced onion, ½ cup of melted butter, salt and pepper to taste. Mix well and form into a loaf. Put a tablespoonful of melted butter in a pan, lay in the loaf, bake 1½ hours, basting often and adding water if dry. Make brown gravy to serve with it.
Mrs. O. H. Ward.

SALMON A LA CREME.

Boil 1 pint of cream, mix one tablespoonful of flour, heaping, in cold milk, with parsley and a small white

---

VALENTINES VARNISHES **VALENTINE & COMPANY,** Coach and Car Varnishes and Colors.

onion and put it in the milk. Let it boil a few minutes, then strain out the onion and parsley and add 1 tablespoonful of butter. Butter a deep dish and fill it with alternate layers of flaked salmon, salt, pepper and the dressing. Sprinkle bread crumbs over the top and bake 1 hour. Mrs. A. C. Guion.

FOR LUNCHEON.

Round steak nearly an inch thick. Cut in small pieces about an inch square. Put a layer of meat in the bottom of a baking dish. Season with pepper and salt and dredge *thickly* with flour. Repeat, seasoning and dredging each layer, until the dish is about ⅔ full. Cover with water which has been seasoned with ½ cup of tomato juice, or ½ teaspoonful of Worcestershire sauce, or a little onion. Cover and bake 2 hours in a moderate oven. Mrs. H. L. Humphrey.

CUCUMBER AND SHRIMP.

A CREOLE RECIPE.

Use 4 short, thick cucumbers and 1 can of shrimp. Mince shrimp very fine; add 4 common soda crackers, rolled very fine; 3 tablespoonfuls of melted butter, a pinch of cayenne pepper, ½ cupful of milk and a pinch of salt, if necessary. Halve the cucumbers, scoop out the seeds and add to the shrimp mixture. Fill the cucumber shells with the mixture, adding a little water, if not moist enough. Sprinkle with cracker crumbs and place in the oven 20 minutes. Put a whole shrimp on the top for effect. MRS. F. W. NORWOOD.

SALMON IN A MOULD.

Drain the liquor from 1 can of salmon, and remove the bones and skin. Chop fine and rub into it until smooth, 4 tablespoonfuls of melted butter, season with salt, pepper and minced parsley, also a little celery, if liked. Beat 4 eggs well, add ½ cupful of cracker crumbs, mix all well and thoroughly. Put into a buttered mould and steam one hour.

SAUCE.

Boil 1 cupful of milk and thicken with 1 tablespoonful of corn starch; add to the liquor from the salmon, 1 tablespoonful of butter, 1 egg, and 1 teaspoonful of catsup. Put the egg in last and very carefully. Boil 1 minute. Turn the salmon out of the mold and pour the sauce around. MRS. L. B. MASON.

TURBOT OR ESCALLOPED FISH.

Steam or boil a large whitefish with 2 bay leaves, 4 cloves and a small sliced onion, until the fish is done;

VALENTINE'S VARNISHES **VALENTINE & COMPANY,** Coach and Car Varnishes and Colors.

about ½ an hour. Boil 1 pint of milk, thicken with 2 tablespoonfuls of flour, and add ¼ pound of butter, salt, pepper and minced parsley. When cool add 2 beaten eggs. Pick the fish to pieces, laying it in a buttered dish, covering each layer with the sauce, until the dish is full; cover the top with bread crumbs, dot thickly with bits of butter and bake until brown.

Mrs. Elmer Washburn.

LYONNAISE POTATOES.

Cut into cubes enough cold boiled potatoes to make 1 quart, add 1 large teaspoonful salt and ⅓ of pepper. Put 3 tablespoonfuls butter into frying pan, add 1 tablespoonful minced onion and 1 of minced parsley, cook 3 minutes, stirring constantly; add the potatoes and stir with a fork, very carefully, until brown and hot.

Mrs. Homer P. Knapp.

CHICKEN SOUFFLE.

Put 1 tablespoonful of butter in a saucepan and when melted, stir in 1 tablespoonful of flour until smooth, add 1 pint of milk and stir until it boils. Add ½ cup of stale bread crumbs; cook 1 minute. Take from the fire, add ½ teaspoonful of salt, 2 dashes of pepper, 1

A. N. Warner & Co. } NOTIONS, 53rd St. & Lake Ave., Chicago

tablespoonful of chopped parsley, 1 can of chopped chicken and the well beaten yolks of 3 eggs. Beat the whites to a stiff froth and stir them in, carefully. Butter a baking dish, pour in this mixture and bake 20 minutes; serve quickly. MRS. B. R. WELLS.

EGG PLANT, FRENCH STYLE.

Boil a large egg plant until tender, peel and mash smooth, season with butter, pepper, salt and a little thyme. Chop fine 2 hard boiled eggs and ½ an onion, add 2 tablespoonfuls of bread crumbs. Mix well, put into buttered dish, put bread crumbs over the top with bits of butter and bake in quick oven until brown.

MRS. WALTER R. COMSTOCK.

TOMATOES WITH EGGS, SPANISH STYLE.

Put 3 tablespoonfuls of tomatoes in pan, add an onion, cut fine, a little parsley, salt and pepper, let it simmer. Fry eggs in another pan, basting them with the butter. Place the eggs on a platter and pour the sauce over. MRS. F. H. WAIT.

SCALLOPED SWEET POTATOES.

A SOUTHERN RECIPE.

Parboil sweet potatoes (yams preferred) and cut in transverse slices; cover the bottom of a pudding dish

with these. Add a little butter, a little sugar and nutmeg. Strew over this a very few bits of orange peel, and add a little juice of the orange. Fill the dish in this manner. Bake about half an hour. A dish fit for an epicure.   Mrs. A. W. Knight.

BAKED CORN OR CORN PUDDING.

Cut kernels off 12 ears of tender uncooked corn, add yolks and whites, beaten separately, of 4 eggs, 1 teaspoonful of sugar, same of flour, mixed with tablespoonful butter, salt and pepper and 1 pint milk. Bake about ½ or ¾ of an hour.   Mrs. Florence Chapman.

BAKED SALMON.

Add to 1 pint salmon 2 beaten eggs, 3 tablespoonfuls of cream, salt and pepper. Put in a dish, set in a pan of water and bake 20 minutes. Turn out on a hot platter, garnish with potato balls and pour around it a sauce made of 1 tablespoonful of butter, 1 of flour and 1 cup of boiling milk; add a tablespoon of chopped parsley.

SANDWICHES.

Yolks of 4 hard boiled eggs powdered very fine with a fork, ¾ cup of butter warmed just enough to pour, 1

A. N. Warner & Co.   HOSIERY,
53rd St. & Lake Ave., Chicago

teaspoonful of mustard. Mix thoroughly and spread the bread with this mixture. Have the whites chopped very fine and well mixed with 1 can of potted ham. Put this between the slices. Very fine for parties.

Mrs. Anna W. Knight.

EGG TIMBALES.

Beat 6 eggs, 1 teaspoonful of chopped parsley, 1 of salt, ¼ of onion juice, pepper to taste, mix thoroughly together, and add 3 gills of milk. Pour the mixture into buttered moulds and stand them in pan of boiling water, up to the edge. Bake 20 minutes, or until firm in middle.

SAUCE FOR ABOVE.

Put 3 tablespoonfuls of butter in saucepan, add 2 tablespoonfuls of flour, stir until smooth, gradually add 1 pint of milk, stir until it boils, add 1 teaspoonful of salt, ¼ of pepper, 4 drops of onion juice and 1 tablespoonful of minced parsley. Mrs. J. E. Hayes.

CORN OMELET.

Beat the yolks of 5 eggs until thick and add 1 gill of milk or cream, stir into 1 pint of grated corn, season with salt, beat the whites well, and stir in lightly. Put

VALENTINE'S VARNISHES VALENTINE & COMPANY, Coach and Car Varnishes and Colors.

3 tablespoonfuls of butter in a fry pan and when hot, add the mixture; fry light brown and turn over.

Mrs. D. H. Champlin.

EGG NESTS.

Beat the whites of as many eggs as you wish to serve and put the beaten white of each egg on a slice of toast, leaving a hole in the center. Into this, put butter, salt and pepper, with the yolk of an egg on top. Set in the oven until brown. Garnish with parsley.

Mrs. R. P. Lamont.

EGG VERMICELLI.

Boil 3 eggs 20 minutes, separate the yolks and chop the whites fine. Toast 4 slices of bread, cut ½ into squares and ½ into triangles. Make a sauce of 1 cup of cream or milk, 1 teaspoonful of butter, 1 (heaping) of flour, ½ of salt, 1 saltspoonful of pepper. Stir the whites into the sauce and while hot, pour it over the toast. Rub the yolks through a fine strainer over the whole, garnish with toast triangles and put a bit of parsley in the center. Miss Edith A. Stevens.

CAULIFLOWER.

A new way of cooking cauliflower. Divide the

A. N. Warner & Co.} Underwear.

vegetable into little boquets and cook in salted water. Strain and cool. Season with salt, white pepper, chopped parsley and sprinkle with flour. Dip in beaten egg and plunge into boiling lard.

BOSTON SANDWICHES.

Boil 1 pint of chestnuts and 2 large chicken livers until tender. Remove the brown skin from the nuts by pouring over them boiling water after they are shelled. Pound to a paste and season with salt, lemon juice and pepper. Spread upon thin slices of white bread.

MRS. J. E. BROWN.

BEACH SAUSAGES.

Two pounds of veal, ½ pound of fat salt pork, chopped very fine. Add 1 pint of oysters and chop. Dredge in a little flour and pepper and fry.

MRS. M. E. BROWN.

LUNCHEON NEST.

Chop fine whatever cold meat, fowl or fish you have Season and add half as much again mashed potato; moisten with gravy, if possible, or rich milk; mold into egg shape, then dip into beaten egg, roll in cracker or bread crumbs; fry a delicate brown. Fill a hot dish with enough fried potatoes, sliced like straws, to represent a nest. Lay your croquettes in this and serve at once. S. F. A.

VALENTINES VARNISHES **VALENTINE & COMPANY,** Coach and Car Varnishes and Colors.

LUNCHEON.

OYSTER SHORTCAKE.

Make a rich but delicate shortcake dough, using sweet milk and Cameo baking powder. Bake in jelly cake tins, in rather thin layers and lightly butter each as it comes from the oven. Drain 1 quart of oysters, putting the liquor on to scald. Heat a cup and a half of milk and a tablespoonful of butter. Rub smooth a tablespoonful of flour in a little cold milk, and add this to the scalding milk, stirring until it thickens. If half a cup of cream can be had add it to the milk; it is a great improvement. Put a teaspoonful of butter into the oyster juice after it is skimmed, salt and pepper to taste, add the oysters, let them scald until they "ruffle," which will be very soon. Then take them out, lay them on a layer of shortcake; pour the juice into the milk, stir well, put a spoonful of this filling over the oysters, lay on another layer of shortcake, then add more oysters, pouring the hot filling over the whole. The dish should be very hot, and it should not stand a minute after being prepared and served. If the cakes are very thin and crisp, three layers may be used instead of two.　　　　Selected.

SAUSAGE DUMPLINGS.

Cook some sausages until thoroughly done, but do not brown too much. Then roll out a crust; cut in squares. On each square lay a sausage; fold the corners across, pressing them together. Then place in a pan and bake in

A. N. Warner & Co. } DRESSMAKING SUPPLIES.

a hot oven until the crust is done. Place on a hot plate and pour the sausage fryings, to which has been added a little water, around the cakes in the dish.

CAULIFLOWER AU GRATIN.

Dress 1 large-sized or 2 small-sized cauliflowers. Place in a saucepan with a tablespoonful of salt and ½ dozen peppercorns; cover with cold water; boil half an hour; drain and place in a baking dish. Pour over a pint of cream sauce, with 3 tablespoonfuls of grated cheese stirred in. Sprinkle 3 tablespoonfuls more over the top, then a light layer of bread crumbs. Set in a brisk oven for about 20 minutes, or until a rich golden brown.

A FRIEND.

CODFISH IN CREAM.

Shred and soak ½ cup of salted codfish over night. In the morning drain, place in a stewpan, cover with cold water; when it boils, drain; cover again with water and simmer gently 15 minutes; add 1 cup of rich milk. Rub 1 spoonful of flour smooth in 1 spoonful of butter; add to the codfish; mince 1 hard-boiled egg, stir into the mixture; add a pinch of pepper and a teaspoonful of minced parsley. Boil up once. Serve.

MRS. WILSON.

LUNCHEON.

RUMBLED EGGS.

Take a small teaspoonful of butter and 2 of cream or milk, warm in a frying-pan. Break 4 eggs, or more if needed, in the pan and stir until slightly cooked; then add 4 sardines broken in small pieces, from which the skin and large bones have been removed. Pour over ½ teaspoonful of Worcestershire sauce and serve hot. A good recipe for cooking in a chafing dish.

BIRD'S-NEST TOAST.

Separate the white of 1 egg from the yolk, leaving yolk unbroken. Beat the white to a stiff froth and lay in circular form on a flat pan. Drop yolk of egg in center of white and place in oven, allowing it to brown slowly. Dust with salt and pepper and serve on hot dish, allowing 5 eggs and 5 slices of toast to each 5 persons.

"DEVIL" FOR SLICES OF GOOSE.

Scald 1 cup of milk; while it is scalding mix with a heaped tablespoonful of bread crumbs, 1 teaspoonful of made mustard, ½ teaspoonful of salt, ¼ teaspoonful of pepper; add to this 1 large tablespoonful of butter and 1 teaspoonful of catsup. Rub 1 tablespoonful of flour and 1 of butter together and stir into the scalding milk; when it thickens add gradually to the other mixture, and lastly, 1 beaten yolk of egg. Return to the fire, heat through, remove at once and spread on each slice of goose.

Miss M. E. Wright.

EGG FLOWERS.

Toast as many pieces of bread as there are persons. Dip an instant into hot cream and place on a hot platter while the eggs are preparing. Put a tablespoonful of lard into an iron skillet; let it become very hot. Break each egg carefully into a saucer and slip into the smoking fat. When the white is set tip the skillet slightly and baste the eggs with the hot grease until the yolks are covered with a thin white veil. Take up carefully and place an egg on each slice of toast. Season lightly with salt and pepper. Garnish with parsley.

OYSTERS AND MACARONI.

Boil macaroni in salted water until done, then put a layer of it in a deep dish and over this a thick layer of oysters. Season with butter, cayenne pepper, salt and a little grated lemon rind. Add a gill of cream or milk to a quart dish. Strew top with bread crumbs and butter, and bake in a quick oven.

VALENTINES VARNISHES   **VALENTINE & COMPANY,**
Coach and Car Varnishes and Colors.

LUNCHEON POTATOES.

Into a tablespoonful of butter made hot stir $\frac{1}{4}$ of an onion and brown it; add 2 cups cold potatoes chopped or thinly sliced and let them brown. Just before taking them up sprinkle them with a quarter teaspoonful each of salt and dry mustard.

CURRIED EGGS.

Boil 4 eggs half an hour, remove the shells and slice eggs into a shallow dish; fry 1 teaspoonful chopped onion in a tablespoonful of butter, being careful not to burn; add 1 heaping tablespoonful of flour and $\frac{1}{2}$ tablespoonful of curry powder, pour on slowly 1 cup of milk, season with salt and pepper and a piece of butter the size of a walnut, simmer until onions are soft, then pour the mixture over the sliced eggs, cover with a layer of bread crumbs, brown in the oven and serve hot.

CRACKER OMELET.

Break 1 quart of oyster crackers into small pieces, pour over them 1 pint of hot milk, with half teaspoonful salt; stir in 3 eggs well beaten and put into a hot buttered skillet. Cook slowly ten minutes, stirring frequently.

Chop together fine 1 pound veal and 1 pint oysters; season with salt and pepper and fry in hot butter.

A. N. Warner & Co. } **GLOVES.**

CHEESE FRITTERS.

Mix 2 tablespoonfuls of grated cheese with 2 dessertspoonfuls of bread crumbs, ½ teaspoonful of dry mustard, a dessertspoonful of butter, a speck of cayenne and the yolk of an egg; pound with a potato masher till smooth and well mixed, make into balls the size of small walnuts, flatten a little. Make a batter with a cup of sifted flour, a tablespoonful of melted butter, a scant cup of warm water, salt to taste and the white of an egg well beaten. Drop the fritters onto this and then from a spoon into very hot fat, cooking as you would croquettes. A. M. D.

PERFECTION SALSIFY.

Boil the roots, after scraping, in salted water until tender. Mash fine, adding a large spoonful of fresh butter, salt and pepper and the beaten yolk of 1 egg; flour to make stiff as for fritters. Beat thoroughly; drop by the spoonful into hot lard and fry a delicate brown. By making them just moist enough to handle, shaping them like oysters, and rolling them in salted cracker dust before frying, the oyster delusion is well-nigh complete.

CHESTNUT CROQUETTES.

Use 50 chestnuts, 2 gills of cream, 3 tablespoonfuls of butter, saltspoon of salt, 4 eggs and some sifted bread crumbs for breading. Shell the chestnuts, put into a stew-

VALENTINE & COMPANY,
Coach and Car Varnishes and Colors

pan with enough water to cover them. Boil 30 minutes. Drain off the water and pound the nuts until very fine; add 1 tablespoonful of the butter and pound until well mixed; add balance of butter and the salt and pound 10 minutes, then add the cream, a little at a time. When it is all worked in rub the mixture through a sieve. Beat 3 eggs until light and stir into that which has been strained. Place in a double boiler and cook 8 minutes, stirring constantly. It should by this time be smooth and thick, if the water in the outer boiler has been boiling rapidly. Spread on a large platter to cool. When cold butter the hands and mold into balls or cones. Dip into the fourth egg, then into the bread crumbs; fry a minute and a half. Arrange on a warm napkin and serve. MRS. BATES.

TRIPE A LA CONTANCE.

One pound of thin tripe, ½ pound of bacon, 1 small carrot, juice of ½ lemon, 1 small onion, bouquet garni, parsley, 2 ounces of butter, 1 tablespoonful of Worcestershire sauce, 1 ounce of flour, 1 pint of stock. Wash the tripe in cold water and then blanch it—that is, put it on in cold water and let it come to a boil—take it out of the stew pan, throw the water away, dry it with a clean cloth and cut it into strips 2 inches wide and 4 inches long. Cut the bacon into very thin slices the same size as the strips of tripe. Chop up the parsley fine, lay the strips of bacon on

A. N. Warner & Co.} LACES.

the tripe, sprinkle a little parsley on each, roll them up together and tie round with string. Cut up the onion and carrot and put them with the bouquet garni into a stewpan with the rolls of tripe and 1 pint of stock, and let all simmer for 2 hours, then take out the rolls of tripe. Mix 2 ounces of butter and 1 ounce of flour together in a stewpan, strain the stock into it, stir till it thickens, add the lemon juice and Worcestershire sauce, also the rolls of tripe, long enough to get hot through. Arrange the tripe in a circle around mashed potatoes and pour the sauce around.

SELECTED.

FISH OMELET.

Cook together 1 level tablespoonful of flour and 1 of butter; add gradually ½ cup of hot milk and a little pepper. Pour boiling water on a ½ cup of shredded codfish, drain and mix with the thickened milk, then add 2 cups of cold boiled potatoes chopped fine. Melt tablespoonful of butter in a spider; when hot turn in fish and cook slowly until a thick crust has formed; then fold over and serve on hot platter.

A. R.

LITTLE PIGS IN BLANKETS.

Season large oysters with salt and pepper. Cut fat English bacon in very thin slices, wrap an oyster in each

---

VALENTINES VARNISHES **VALENTINE & COMPANY,** Coach and Car Varnishes and Colors.

slice and fasten with a wooden toothpick. Heat a frying pan and put in the little pig. Cook just long enough to crisp the bacon, about two minutes. Place on slices of toast that have been cut into small pieces. Do not remove the skewers; garnish with parsley. Have the pan very hot before the pigs are put in and shake continually; do not not burn.

EGGS POACHED IN MILK.

Three pints of milk in a porcelain-lined skillet heated to a boiling point. Break your eggs into the poacher, set in the skillet and cook slowly on the back of the range until firm. The milk neutralizes the sulphur of the eggs, making them much more wholesome to people of bilious temperament.

POTATO HILLOCKS.

Whip boiled potatoes very light; to a pint of mashed potato add a scant tablespoonful of butter, a tablespoonful of hot milk or cream, $\frac{1}{2}$ teaspoonful of salt, $\frac{1}{4}$ teaspoonful of pepper. Beat in a raw egg, shape into small conical heaps; put in a greased pan on a hot oven, and as they brown glaze them with butter. Have the oven very hot; also have a very hot platter. Slip a cake-turner under each one and transfer to the hot dish.

A. N. Warner & Co.} Embroideries.

LUNCHEON.

GRAS A L'AMERICAINE.

Boil 2 pounds of calf's liver until very tender; save the juice. Pick the liver over, pulling out all the strings and fat. Mash with potato masher to pulp, adding gradually the juice from the liver. Add 2 tablespoofuls of melted butter, salt to taste, a little cayenne, juice of 2 lemons, ½ teaspoonful of allspice; ½ of cinnamon, ½ of cloves. Put it into a mold and let it stand in a cold place 24 hours. Slice and serve. MISS CLARA WILLIAMS.

POTATO TIMBAL.

Pare 8 good sized potatoes, cover with boiling water and cook 30 minutes. Drain and mash smooth and light. Add 3 tablespoonfuls of butter, 2 of finely chopped parsley, salt and pepper to taste. Gradually beat into this 1 cup of milk, hot; stir hard and beat in 3 well beaten eggs. Butter an oval basin and cover it thickly with fine crumbs, fill with the prepared potato and bake in a moderate oven ½ hour. Let the dish stand a few minutes after taking from the oven then invert upon a hot platter. J. S. P.

BAKED RICE WITH TOMATOES.

Boil 1 cup of rice till tender, when done mix with a can of tomatoes. Add a little onion chopped very fine and

---

VALENTINES VARNISHES **VALENTINE & COMPANY,** Coach and Car Varnishes and Colors.

a small piece of butter. Season with pepper and salt to taste. Put in a well buttered dish, lined with bread crumbs and bake to a golden brown.

FRIED TOMATOES.

Slice fresh ripe tomatoes in half, sprinkle a little salt and pepper over each piece and roll in flour. Put butter in frying pan and when hot put in tomatoes with skin side down, turn, and when cooked make a gravy by pouring over them milk, and simmer, till thick. A green pepper, sliced and fried with them improves the flavor.

EGG-PLANT.

One large egg-plant, 3 eggs, well beaten, 4 or 5 crackers, rolled fine, 1 tablespoonful of chopped onion, 1 of celery, butter the size of a walnut. Boil egg-plant in salt water till tender. Beat well and add ingredients. Put in a well-buttered mold and bake.

Mrs. S. E. Bagshawe.

STUFFED EGGS.

Boil 6 eggs 20 minutes, remove the shells and cut carefully lengthwise. Remove the yolks and put the whites of each egg separate, so they will fit nicely. Mash the yolks and add 1 teaspoonful of soft butter, half as much

---

A. N. Warner & Co.} Fancy Goods.

LUNCHEON.

deviled ham as you have egg. Season to taste with pepper, mustard and a little vinegar. Fill the whites with the mixture, smooth them and press the two halves together. Spread the remainder of the yolks on a shallow dish and place the eggs on it. Cover with a thin white sauce. Sprinkle buttered bread crumbs over the whole and bake until a delicate brown. This is a fine dish for Sunday tea.

Mrs. T. J. Hudson.

VEAL CROQUETTES.

Chop fine some cold veal; season highly with salt, pepper, onion juice, celery salt and parsley. Moisten with beaten egg and white sauce, shape in rolls. Roll in bread crumbs, then in beaten egg and again in the crumbs. These are nice for luncheon, served with peas. If canned peas are used, pour off half the liquor in the can. Add milk, let them boil, season with butter, pepper and salt. Thicken a little with flour.

Mrs. T. J. Hudson.

VALENTINES VARNISHES   **VALENTINE & COMPANY,**
Coach and Car Varnishes and Colors.

DESSERTS.

"There is a *knack* in doing many a thing
Which labor cannot to perfection bring;
Therefore, however great in your own eyes,
Pray do not hints from other folks despise."

SAUCE FOR PLUM PUDDING.

Cream together 1 cup of sugar and ½ cup of butter. When light and creamy add the well-beaten yolks of 4 eggs. Stir into this 1 wine glass of brandy, a pinch of salt, and 1 large cupful of hot cream or rich milk. Beat this mixture well, place it in a saucepan over the fire, stir until it cooks sufficiently to thicken like cream. Be sure and do not let it boil. *Delicious.*   Mrs. G. W. Hoyt.

DANISH PUDDING.

Soak 1 cup of tapioca all night. Cook 1 hour in double boiler with 3 pints of water, stirring often. Add ½ teaspoonful of salt, ½ teacupful of sugar, a tumbler of bright jelly; mix thoroughly, mould, and when hardened, serve with cream.   Mrs. Chas. A. Knorr.

A. N. Warner & Co.} Trunks.

MINCE PIE MEAT.

Boil and chop fine 2 pounds of beef, powder and free from strings 1 pound of suet, pare and chop 5 pounds of apples, 2 pounds of raisins (seeded), 1 pound of Sultana raisins, 2 pounds of currants, ¾ pound of citron, 2 large oranges, 2½ pounds of brown sugar, 2 lemons, juice of both and grated rind of 1, 2 tablespoonfuls of cinnamon, 2 of mace, 1 of cloves, 1 of allspice, 1 of fine salt, 1 quart of sherry wine, 1 pint of brandy, 1 teaspoonful of nutmeg, enough good cider and syrup from pickled fruit to thoroughly moisten the mixture.   MRS. J. B. DANIELS.

WHIPPED PEACHES.

Beat 1 cup of chopped peaches with ½ cup of sugar and the beaten white of 1 egg for a half hour. Serve ice cold with cream.   MRS. C. J. SWAN.

MOCK PINEAPPLE.

Pare, core and slice crosswise rather thinly 2 nice apples. Pare and remove white skin from 3 nice oranges, slicing them crosswise, and lay a slice of the apple upon 1 of the orange, saving every drop of juice. Sugar plentifully and squeeze on it the juice of a lemon and a glass of sherry wine. Serve ice cold.

FRUIT COMPOTE.

Pare and chop fine 3 good apples; slice thin 3 bananas; mix together. Boil to a syrup 1 cup of sugar with ½ cup of milk. Flavor with the juice and grated rind of ½ a lemon, pour over the fruit and serve cold.

APPLE JOHN.

Sift 1 pint of flour with 2 teaspoonfuls of Cameo baking powder, add two tablespoonfuls of butter and 1 cup of milk. Pare and cut 1 quart of apples into eighths, put them into a deep pie-plate, lay the crust over and bake. When done, invert it upon a large plate and season well with sugar, butter and spice. H. M. W.

ROSE PUDDING.

Scald 1 quart of milk in a double boiler and add 5 tablespoonfuls of sifted flour, mixed smooth in cold milk with a pinch of salt. Stir well and boil until thick, then add 4 well-beaten eggs. Flavor with 3 or 4 drops of strong rose extract. Pour into mould, and when cold and firm turn out and surround with a rim of berries of some kind. Serve with sugar and cream.

Mrs. C. J. Swan.

FESTINA DESSERT.

Take 1 quart can of best blackberries, or a quart of fresh ones, and set in a cold place while 4 soda crackers

---

A. N. Warner & Co.} Valises.

are being crushed to a fine powder by the rolling pin. Place upon the table in separate dishes. Serve by putting the berries upon a saucer, covering with a dessert spoonful of the cracker powder, and eat with cream and sugar, if desired. MRS. TENNANT.

OLD MAID'S PUDDING.

Cream ½ cup of sugar with butter the size of 1 egg, add 2 eggs well beaten, a pinch of salt, 2 cups of flour, into which sift 3 teaspoonfuls of Cameo baking powder. Steam or bake.

SAUCE.

Cream ½ cup of butter with 1½ cups of brown sugar, and add 2 tablespoonfuls of flour, put on the fire and add boiling water, stirring until it is thick; add a large cup of black raspberries or the same amount of canned raspberries, and serve immediately. MRS. G. W. HOYT.

CARAMEL CUSTARD.

Dissolve 1 cup of granulated sugar in an iron saucepan until it scorches a little. Add ½ cup of water and melt until like a thin brown syrup.

Make a custard of 1 quart of milk, 4 eggs well beaten and a pinch of salt. Add the above syrup and bake in cups set into water in a dripping pan.

MRS. M. W. HARTWELL.

VALENTINE & COMPANY,
Coach and Car Varnishes and Colors.

DESSERTS.

STUFFED DATE PUDDING.

Remove seeds from ¼ pound of dates, and stuff with chopped nuts. Make a custard of 1 quart milk, yolks 4 eggs, 1 tablespoonful corn starch, 1 teaspoonful vanilla. Put in a baking dish and bake for ten minutes. Remove from oven and cover the top with the stuffed dates and a meringue made of the whites of 4 eggs and 4 table- four tablespoonfuls of pulverized sugar. Return to the oven and brown the meringue. MRS. JOSEPH GREGG.

GRAHAM PUDDING.

Two cups graham flour, 1 cup molasses, 1 cup sweet milk, 1 cup chopped raisins, 1 small teaspoonful soda; steam three hours. Serve with hot sauce, any flavor desired. MRS. A. E. COLEMAN.

FANCY PUDDING.

Soak 1 box gelatine in 1 pint sherry, add 1 pint boiling water and 1 cup sugar. Put in a mold, and when beginning to stiffen add 2 oranges sliced, 1 bananna sliced, a few figs, cut, ¼ pound candied cherries, and if liked, ¼ pound chocolate creams. Serve with whipped cream sweetened and flavored with wine. A. W. K.

NICE PLAIN PUDDING.

Three eggs well beaten, 3 tablespoonfuls sugar, 2

of butter, 1 cup sweet milk, 1 of raisins, 1 teaspoonful Cameo baking powder, flour to make as thick as cake; steam 30 minutes. Serve with sauce.

MRS. V. M. HARPER.

IMPERIAL PUDDING.

Wash ½ cup rice, put on to boil in 1 quart cold water. When it begins to boil, pour off all the water and add 1 pint milk. Cook in a double boiler 1 hour. Then add ½ box gelatine soaked in ½ cup of water; 1 cup sugar, ½ teaspoonful of salt, 4 tablespoonfuls of wine. Stir in rice till thick, then add 1 quart cream, (whipped). Serve with the following strawberry sauce : Beat ½ pint of thick cream till *very* thick, add ½ cup jam. Sweeten to taste.

MISS GERTRUDE A. HUBBARD.

SWISS CREAM.

Boil 1 pint cream with rind of 2 lemons cut very thin and ½ cup sugar. Mix the juice of the lemon with a heaping teaspoonful of flour and pour upon it the boiling cream, stirring all the time. When nearly cold pour it over 6 maccaroons which have been dipped in wine. Serve very cold. If the lemons are large and quite juicy, 1 will be enough.

MRS. EARL W. SPENCER.

VALENTINES VARNISHES VALENTINE & COMPANY, Coach and Car Varnishes and Colors.

DESSERTS.

ENGLISH PLUM PUDDING.

Chop fine ½ pound suet. Add 1 pound sugar, 1 pound eggs, 1 of raisins, 2 of currants, ½ of flour, ½ of bread crumbs, 1 pint milk, 1 glass brandy, 1 of wine, 2 nutmegs, 2 tablespoonfuls of ginger, little salt and cinnamon. Tie in a bag and boil 6 hours.

Mrs. J. P. Montross.

APPLE CITRON PIE.

To make 1 pie, take 3 tablespoonfuls of flour and 1 of lard, with 1 teaspoonful of salt; mix with ice water, rather dry. Line the pie plate with crust, and fill with sliced apples, sprinkling over them 1 ounce of finely cut citron; add 3 tablespoonfuls of sugar and 1 teaspoonful of butter in small bits. Cover with crust and bake in moderate oven.

PRUNE PIE.

Soak ¾ of a pound of prunes all night in water enough to cover, cook until tender and but little juice; pit them. Line the pie plate with crust, put in prunes, ¼ of a cup of sugar, 1 teaspoonful of butter in bits, grated rind and juice of ½ a lemon, a little salt and a sprinkling of flour. Cover and bake ½ hour.

A. N. Warner & Co.} Perfumery.

DESSERTS.

APPLE COBBLER.

Slice juicy cooking apples and fill a small biscuit pan. Strew over bits of butter, 3 large spoonfuls of sugar, nutmeg, cinnamon to taste, and add ½ cup of water. Make a crust of ½ pint of flour, ½ tablespoonful of butter and lard mixed, a little salt and 1 teaspoonful of Cameo baking powder mixed with ice water to a soft dough, spread the crust over the apples and bake in moderate oven. Invert upon a platter and serve with the following sauce:

SAUCE.

One dessertspoonful of butter, 3 tablespoonfuls of brown sugar, 1 cup of boiling water, 1 heaping teaspoonful of corn starch, flavor with vanilla or wine.

MRS. JOHN UNDERWOOD.

COCOANUT PIE.

Cream ½ cup of butter with 2 of sugar, add 2 cups of milk and 2 grated cocoanuts; 4 eggs. Flavor with lemon extract. Bake in open shells of paste.

MRS. J. S. SARGENT.

LEMON PIE.

Beat the yolks of 3 eggs with the juice and grated rind of a large lemon, add ½ cup of sugar, 1 cup of milk, 1 teaspoonful of corn starch dissolved in milk.

VALENTINE'S VARNISHES VALENTINE & COMPANY, Coach and Car Varnishes and Colors.

DESSERTS.

Beat the whites of the eggs with 4 teaspoonfuls of powdered sugar for the meringue and spread over and brown when the pie is baked.   Mrs. J. B. Daniels.

MILK SHERBET.

One quart of milk, 1 pint of sugar, juice of 4 lemons, or a pint of mashed strawberries. Put milk in freezer, freeze 20 minutes, stir in sugar and fruit juice; freeze.   Mrs. W. H. French.

ICE CREAM.

Heat 1 quart of milk to boiling, add 2 heaping tablespoonfuls of corn starch, wet with cold milk and cook until thick. When cool add 1 quart of cream, 2 cups of sugar and flavoring.   Mrs. W. E. Ritchie.

EMMA HARDY'S RECIPE FOR ICE CREAM.

Two quarts of cream, 2 cups of sugar, 2 eggs, whites and yolks beaten separately, 1 tablespoonful of flavoring. Boil one cup of the cream, dissolve 1 teaspoonful of Bermuda arrowroot in a little cold milk and stir it into the hot cream. Thicken, remove from the fire and stir it into the cold cream, add sugar and flavoring and the beaten yolks. Strain and put into freezer. Do not turn the crank for 15 minutes, then stir in the beaten whites and beat the whole well. Remove the dasher and set aside for 2 hours. At the end of an hour loosen

---

A. N. Warner & Co.} Linings.

the cream from the sides and beat again. In making chocolate cream, omit the arrowroot. In making strawberry, omit the yolks of the eggs, use 1 quart of cream, and when partly frozen add 1 quart of strawberry juice. Apple sauce strained and the beaten whites of eggs and sugar added is delicious.

SHERBET.

One pint of fruit juice, 1 pint of sugar, 1 pint of water in which 1 tablespoonful of Knox's gelatine has been properly dissolved. Freeze same as cream.

Mrs. I. M. Bennett.

ICES.

One pint of the strongest coffee, 1 pint of richest cream. Sweeten and freeze.

Mrs. W. H. French.

One quart of rich cream, 1 quart of crushed raspberries. Sweeten and freeze.

Mrs. W. H. French.

FROZEN PUNCH.

Boil 1 quart of water with 1 quart of sugar to a thick syrup, pour it over 1 quart of chopped pineapple, while boiling. Let this stand over night. Next day add the juice of 4 lemons and the whites of 4 eggs,

DESSERTS.

frothed; add 1 large cup of wine and a tablespoonful of brandy. Freeze.   Mrs. S. P. Douthart.

ICE CREAM.

Mix 1 can of condensed milk with 1 quart of fresh milk; beat the yolks of 2 eggs and add; then the whites, frothed; sweeten to taste, flavor and freeze. If too rich, add milk.   Mrs. Willard.

APPLE FRITTERS.

Two eggs, 1 quart of flour, 1 cup of sugar, ½ cup of currants, 2 even teaspoonfuls of Cameo baking powder, 1½ pints of milk, ½ teaspoonful of cinnamon, ½ of allspice, 1 quart of chopped apples. Make into shape and fry in lard.   Mrs. John A. Grier.

WINE JELLY.

(WITHOUT BOILING.)

One package of Coxe's gelatine. Pour over it 1 pint of cold water, and let it stand 2 hours. Squeeze into it the juice of 6 lemons; add 1½ pounds of sugar, 1 pint of wine and 1 pint of boiling water. Strain and pour into moulds.   Mrs. A. C. Guion.

RAISIN PUFFS.

Two cups of flour, 1 of raisins, ¼ of butter, 1 of milk, 2 eggs, 2 tablespoonfuls of sugar, 3 teaspoon-

---

A. N. Warner & Co.   WASH DRESS GOODS.

fuls of Cameo baking powder. Steam ½ an hour. Eat with liquid sauce.   Mrs. W. C. Ritchie.

FRUIT BALLS.

Chop 2 ounces of suet fine, add 4 ounces of bread-crumbs, white of 1 egg, ½ cup of currants, ½ of chopped raisins and a little citron; form into balls the size of a walnut. If dry, add white of another egg. Drop the balls in boiling water and cook slowly until they rise, lift with skimmer, dish and pour over a rich brandy sauce, in which have been stirred the yolks of 2 eggs.

Selected.

TAPIOCA PUDDING.

Soak 3 tablespoonfuls of tapioca over night, add 1 quart of sweet milk and cook half an hour; beat the yolks of 4 eggs, 1 cup of granulated sugar and 3 tablespoonfuls of grated cocoanut; stir into the tapioca and milk and cook ten minutes. Pour into large pudding dish, cover with the well-beaten whites of 4 eggs, 3 teaspoonfuls of pulverized sugar, sprinkle top with cocoanut and brown slightly in oven. Serve cold.

Miss Blanche Longmire.

APPLE CUSTARD PUDDING.

Four apples, pare and slice them, put in a dish and cover with 1 cup of water, ½ cup of sugar, a little cin-

VALENTINE & COMPANY,
Coach and Car Varnishes and Colors.

namon, and butter the size of an egg; bake until done. Beat 2 eggs, ½ cup of sugar, a little salt, and 1 pint of milk; pour over the apple and bake one-half hour.

Mrs. Harry N. Day.

PERSIAN CREAM.

One quart of sweet milk, ½ box of Coxe's gelatine or ⅓ box of Boston Crystal gelatine (the latter preferred), 1 cup of sugar, 4 eggs. Put milk in double boiler, and when almost boiling hot, add gelatine (dry). Stir until dissolved; then add yolks of eggs and sugar well beaten together. Cook until the consistency of boiled custard. Remove from fire, and add 1 teaspoonful of vanilla and well beaten whites of the eggs. Stir thoroughly. Pour into moulds; serve with cream. Do not use until the day after making. Mrs. O. H. Ward.

VICTORIA MOULD.

Cut some sponge cakes in slices, dip them in white wine or sherry, place them in layers in the center of a mould with jam between each layer, soak ¼ ounce of gelatine in a little cold water, make a custard with the yolks of 4 eggs and a pint of milk, flavored with vanilla; mix while hot with the gelatine, strain and stir occasionally until the custard is cool; then fill the mould, so that when turned out the custard appears as a crust around

---

A. N. Warner & Co.} Table Linins.

DESSERTS.

the cake. When cold turn into a glass dish and garnish with red currant jelly and whipped cream.

MRS. J. H. R. BOND.

TIPSY SQUIRE.

Saturate a thin sponge cake with sherry wine. Ornament the top thickly with split blanched almonds. Pour over it a rich custard made of 1 quart of milk, yolks of 6 eggs, whites of 2, 1 teacupful of sugar. Whip a pint of cream until thick. Put over the cake and custard alternate spoonfuls of the beaten whites of 4 eggs and the whipped cream.

MRS. JOSEPH GREGG.

CIDER JELLY.

One box of gelatine dissolved in 1 pint of cold water; add 1¼ pounds of sugar 1½ pints of cider, juice and grated rind of 1 lemon, 1 pint of boiling water. Strain into moulds.

MRS. E. L. HALE.

WINE JELLY.

Soak 1 box Cox's gelatine in 1 pint of cold water ½ hour, add 1½ pints of boiling water and ½ pound cut loaf, juice of 3 lemons, 1 quart bottle of sherry wine and the whites of 2 eggs, well beaten, and with the shells stir in the mixture to clarify it. Let it come to a boil, strain and mould.

MRS. H. W. BRIDGE.

VALENTINES VARNISHES VALENTINE & COMPANY, Coach and Car Varnishes and Colors

TAPIOCA CREAM.

Soak 3 tablespoonfuls of tapioca in water all night. Put this into 1 quart of milk and boil half an hour. Beat the yolks of 4 eggs with 1 cup of sugar, add 3 tablespoonfuls of fresh grated cocoanut, add to the milk and boil 10 minutes longer. Beat the whites of the eggs stiff and add 3 tablespoonfuls of powdered sugar. Put this over the top and sprinkle over it 3 tablespoonfuls of cocoanut, and slightly brown in the oven. Serve very cold.   MRS. C. W. CHANDLER.

A BEAUTIFUL DESSERT.

Put 1 quart of milk on the fire, and while heating, mix 5 small tablespoonfuls of corn starch, 4 of sugar, and 4 of grated chocolate, with a little cold milk, add to the hot milk and stir until it thickens. Pour into a mould and cool. Make a boiled custard with 1 quart of milk, 5 eggs, leaving out the whites of 2, and 2 tablespoonfuls of sugar. Pour this, when cold, around the former mixture in a shallow dish. Beat the whites of the 2 eggs left out with two tablespoonfuls of pulverized sugar, and drop from a spoon over the pudding and custard, shaping like kisses; a little bright jelly may be laid upon each kiss, or part of the egg froth colored with fruit syrup and a little piece put upon the top.

MRS. JOHN A. GRIER.

A. N. Warner & Co. MEN'S FURNISHINGS.

DESSERTS.

OLD-FASHIONED BLACKBERRY MUSH.

Put in a kettle 3 quarts of berries, 1 cup of molasses, 1 cup of sugar; when warm add 1 cup of flour, mixed with a little water. Boil 3 to 4 minutes. Serve cold with cream.   MRS. R. P. LAMONT.

LEMON MERINGUE.

One lemon, 1 cup of sugar, 1 cup of water, yolks of 2 eggs, 1 slice of bread without crust, 1 medium tablespoonful of butter. Grate the yellow from the lemon, squeeze the juice and pulp; beat the yolks and sugar together with the bread and lemon. To this add the cup of water, or just enough to fill the pie. Bake with an under crust.   MRS. RUSSELL H. STEVENS.

PEACH COBBLER.

Line side of a pudding dish with pie crust; no bottom crust. Fill with peaches and nearly a pint of cold water, (have some of the peaches whole), and a coffee-cup of light brown sugar. Have a dessert spoonful of flour, well mixed with butter, the size of an egg; place this among the peaches; cover with pie crust; cut slits into it and bake half an hour.
     MRS. W. D. MCKEY.

PRUNE PUDDING.

Cook 3 cups of prunes until tender; when done,

VALENTINE'S VARNISHES   **VALENTINE & COMPANY,**
Coach and Car Varnishes and Colors.

strain juice and all through colander, add 1 cup of sugar, 2 teaspoonfuls of corn starch, stirred together; beat 3 eggs separately, putting in the whites last. Put all into a tin pudding dish; then into a dripping pan filled with water (boiling) and bake ½ hour.

Mrs. B. F. Ray.

STEAMED PUDDING.

One cup of sugar, 3 tablespoonfuls of melted butter, ½ cup of sweet milk, 1 egg, 1½ cups of flour, 2 teaspoonfuls of Cameo baking powder. Steam ¾ of an hour. To be eaten with whipped cream or lemon sauce.

A. E. S.

LEMON SAUCE.
FOR STEAMED PUDDING.

One coffeecup of sugar, small ½ cup of butter, 1 egg, 1 large lemon, all the juice and half the rind, 1 teaspoonful of nutmeg, 3 tablespoonfuls of boiling water. Cream the butter and sugar, and stir in the egg beaten light; the lemon and nutmeg next. Beat hard 10 minutes, and add a teaspoonful at a time the boiling water. Put in a double boiler and let the sauce get hot and thick, but not boil, stirring constantly.

A. E. S.

HEAVENLY HASH.

One-half box of gelatine dissolved in 1½ pints of water, ½ cup of sugar, ⅓ cup of candied cherries, ½ cup of mixed nuts, blanched and chopped, ½ cup of

raisins and citron, mixed; a little vanilla. Boil, and when cold, chop it fine. Serve with whipped cream.
MISS NELLIE HARPER.

FRIAR'S OMELETTE.

Make a sauce with a dozen apples, add ¼ pound of butter, ¼ pound of sugar, 4 eggs. Put into a deep, well-buttered dish, thickly strewn with bread crumbs, in layers, crumbs for the top layer. Add the grated rind and part of the juice of one lemon. When baked turn it out and put sugar over the top. Eat cold with cream.
MRS. W. D. McKEY.

EASY CHARLOTTE.

To every teacup of cream allow the white of 1 egg, and ½ cup of powdered sugar. Keep eggs and cream icy cold. Whip them well, then add the sugar daintily, flavor with vanilla, and pour into a dish lined with pieces of sponge cake or split lady fingers. Put in a cold place to "set." *

PINEAPPLE DESSERT.

Make thin sandwiches of home-made bread and canned grated pineapple. Pour the juice over them and let stand until well soaked, then cover with sweetened whipped cream and serve very cold.
MRS. G. L. PADDOCK.

VALENTINES VARNISHES   **VALENTINE & COMPANY,**
Coach and Car Varnishes and Colors.

DESSERTS.

CARAMEL CUSTARD.

One-half cup of sugar, melted over a slow fire; do not stir it, or touch a cold spoon to it; when a good brown color, add ½ cup of water, *boiling* hot—*bubbling* hot. Simmer 2 or 3 minutes, strain through wire into 1 pint of warm milk, and cool. Beat together 4 eggs, 1 pint of cold milk, 1 teaspoonful of vanilla, a pinch of salt. Add all together and bake slowly, like any other custard. This part can be made the day before using, as it is to be eaten cold. When wanted, cover the dish ½ inch deep with whipped cream. Eat with caramel sauce as follows: One-half cup of sugar, melted and browned, ½ cup of *boiling* water. Simmer 10 minutes. Serve in small pitcher.   Mrs. A. W. Knight.

CHARLOTTE RUSSE.

Whip 1 quart of cream to a stiff froth, whites of 8 eggs, a little less than ½ of a box of gelatine, dissolved in a *very little* water. Stir the froth of the eggs into the cream, sweeten with powdered sugar and flavor with vanilla. Add the gelatine the last thing, then turn into dish lined with lady fingers or slices of sponge cake.

Mrs. Eugene C. Long.

BLANC-MANGE.

Wash a very small handful of Carrageen moss (sold at drug stores), put it in 1 quart of milk. Put in a double boiler and stir frequently, until the moss is nearly dissolved. Strain through cheese-cloth; sweeten to taste

and add vanilla. Put into moulds, and serve with sugar and cream.
MRS. J. B. WHEATLEY.

RICE PUDDING.

Wash in several waters ½ cup of raw rice, put it into 2 quarts of sweet milk with ½ cup of white sugar, a little salt and 1 teaspoonful of vanilla. Bake slowly 2 or 3 hours, stirring every 15 minutes. Eat cold with cream.
MRS. GEORGE L. PADDOCK.

TAPIOCA PUDDING.

Wash 10 tablespoonfuls of tapioca and soak it 3 hours, drain, and put it into 1 quart of rich milk. Set the pan into boiling water and stir until it thickens; add 2 tablespoonfuls of butter, 6 of white sugar, 1 lemon, juice and grated rind (or vanilla extract.)
MRS. WILLIAN L. SHIDE.

APPLE SNOW.

Pare, core, and steam until tender 6 good sized apples. When done put them in a dish, and whip until light; then set aside to cool. When very cold add 1 cup of powdered sugar and juice of 1 lemon. Mix very gently. Beat the whites of 6 eggs to a stiff froth, then add to them by spoonfuls the apples, moving the beater backwards and forwards lightly until the apples and eggs are thoroughly mixed. Serve very cold in glasses.
MRS. JOHN A. GRIER.

VALENTINES VARNISHES **VALENTINE & COMPANY,**
Coach and Car Varnishes and Colors.

DESSERTS.

FRUIT SALAD.

Slice 6 oranges, 6 bananas and 1 pineapple, and mix together. Squeeze the juice of 3 more oranges over. Sprinkle with powdered sugar and add sherry wine, if desired. MRS. IRWIN SIMPSON.

ORANGE SHERBET.

Two or 3 oranges (depends on size and juiciness), 2 cups of pulverized sugar, 3 cups of water, whites of 2 eggs. Grate the rind of 1 orange (if good size) and pour over it 1 cup of boiling water (the sugar may be put in this.) Squeeze the oranges to a pulp and put right in with the water and sugar. Put the rest of the water in cold and strain. Beat the whites of the eggs *very* light and stir in when half frozen. All the water can be boiling and put in if there is plenty of time to cool before freezing. Leave rind in the water until cold.
MRS. RUSSELL H. STEVENS.

SPANISH CREAM.

One pint of milk and ½ box of gelatine heated together, yolks of 3 eggs and 5 tablespoonfuls of sugar beaten together added to the above mixture, remove when it thickens, and stir in the whites of the eggs, beaten to a stiff froth; flavor and put into molds; to be eaten cold with cream. MRS. W. F. PARISH.

DESSERTS. 99

FRUIT SHERBET.

One dozen oranges, 1 dozen bananas, 1½ pounds white grapes, ½ pineapple (preserved), 1 pint cherries (candied or maraschino), 1 pint sherry wine, 2 cups sugar boiled in a little water. The oranges are cut in *dice* shape and mixed with the other fruit. This quantity will serve for 24 persons. MRS. M. N. BURCHARD.

STEAMED GRAHAM PUDDING.

One and a half cups "Akron" graham flour, ¾ cup sweet milk, ½ cup melted butter, ½ cup stoned and chopped raisins, ½ cup currants, ½ cup molasses or sugar, 1 egg, 1 teaspoonful of soda, 1 teaspoonful of cloves, 1 teaspoonful of cinnamon, pinch of salt. Steam 2 hours, serve hot with liquid sherry wine sauce. This is a delicate pudding and dyspeptics can eat it with comfort. MRS. E. B. MYERS.

ENGLISH PLUM PUDDING.

One pound suet chopped fine, 1 pound currants, 1 pound raisins, seeded; 1 pound brown sugar, ½ pound citron, ⅓ pound rolled crackers or bread crumbs, ¼ pound flour, 1 tablespoonful of ground ginger, 1 nutmeg, 1 wineglass of brandy, 8 eggs. Mix well and put

---

VALENTINES VARNISHES   **VALENTINE & COMPANY,** Coach and Car Varnishes and Colors.

DESSERTS.

in mould. Most be kept boiling *constantly* for 5 hours or even longer. Much depends on this point.
       Mrs. A. E. Walker.

OLD ENGLISH PLUM PUDDING.

Beat 10 eggs very light, add 1 pound of sugar and beat well, stir in 1 pound suet finely chopped; next, 1 pound of flour, then 1 pound stoned raisins, 1 pound currants and ½ pound citron, shredded. Add spices to taste, nutmeg, cinnamon and a very little cloves. Lastly, add 1 wineglass of brandy. Tie in a cloth and boil 6 or 7 hours. Eat with brandy sauce.
       Mrs. Walter R. Comstock.

PRESIDENT PUDDING.

Two large tablespoonfuls of butter, 1 cup sugar, yolks of 4 eggs, ½ loaf baker's bread crumbed fine, rind and juice of 1 lemon, 1 teaspoonful of vanilla. Put half this in a small pudding dish, spread on a little preserve, cover with the rest of the pudding. Bake ½ an hour. Make a meringue of the whites of the eggs and 1 cup sugar, vanilla. Brown this. Serve cold. Best the second day. Mrs. E. G. Gilbert.

FIG PUDDING.

One cup of beef suet chopped fine, 1 cup of sugar, yolks of 2 eggs, 1 cup milk, 3 cups of flour, 1 teaspoonful of Cameo baking powder, 1 pound of figs chopped fine, salt. Steam 2 hours. Mrs. F. A. Neal.

PINEAPPLE PUDDING.

One quart milk sweetened and flavored with vanilla, 2 dozen lady fingers separated and dipped in the milk. Lay them in a pudding dish and spread over a layer of grated pineapple, dot it with jelly and fill the dish in this way. Beat the whites of 3 eggs well with 3 tablespoonfuls of sugar, put over the top and brown. Eat with cream if liked.   MRS. M. COCKRILL.

RICE PUDDING.

One cup boiled rice, 3 cups milk, ½ cup sugar, 1 tablespoonful of corn starch, 2 eggs. Flavor with vanilla. Heat the milk in double boiler, dissolve corn starch in cold milk, then stir into hot milk. Beat yolks, add sugar, stir into milk, add rice, and cook until thick like custard, then pour into buttered dish.

MERINGUE.

Beat the whites of 2 eggs stiff, add 2 tablespoonfuls powdered sugar. Put it on top of the pudding, then place it in the oven and brown a little.

MISS EDITH A. STEVENS.

PRUNE PUDDING.

One-half pound of prunes, stewed, stoned and chopped fine, whites of 7 eggs, beaten very light, 7 table-

VALENTINE & COMPANY,
Coach and Car Varnishes and Colors.

spoonfuls of powdered sugar. Mix together, stirring in the prunes last. Bake 40 minutes; to be eaten with cream.
Mrs. B. R. Wells.

PRUNE PUDDING.

One pound of prunes cooked (without sweetening) until tender. Put through colander, then add 1 cup of white sugar; beat hard ½ an hour. Then beat whites of 4 eggs to a stiff froth and add to prunes and eggs, stirring well. Place in a pudding dish and set in a pan of boiling water. Bake in a moderate oven 20 minutes. Serve with whipped cream.
Mrs. Rhodes.

MILK SHERBET.

Three cups of sugar, 3 lemons, 3 pints of milk. Put the milk into the freezer and let it stand until very cold. Mix the sugar and lemon juice, add to the milk and freeze. Serve with candied ginger or fruits, preserved or fresh.

ORANGE TRIFLE.

One pint of whipped cream, 1 cup of powdered sugar, ½ box of gelatine, yolks of 3 eggs, juice of 2 sweet oranges, grated rind of one, 1 cup of boiling water. Mix juice, rind and sugar, pour the hot liquid over. Heat within a vessel of boiling water, stirring constantly to prevent curdling.
Mrs. Rhodes.

DESSERTS.

FROZEN PEACHES.

One can of peaches, 1 heaping pint of sugar, 1 quart of hot water, 2 cups of whipped cream. Boil the sugar and water together 12 minutes, then add the peaches and cook 20 minutes longer; then run through a sieve and cool. Freeze; when nearly frozen remove the cover and add the cream. Let stand one hour before serving. Apricots may be used instead of peaches. MRS. RHODES.

FIG PUDDING.

Six ounces of suet, or 1 full pint, a scant quart of bread crumbs, 4 tablespoofuls of moist sugar, ½ pound of figs, 1 egg, 1 cup of sweet milk, ½ nutmeg. Mix first the bread and suet (chopped fine), then figs (chopped fine) and sugar. Add nutmeg, egg (well beaten) and milk. Steam four hours.

SAUCE FOR FIG PUDDING.

One cup of sugar, ½ cup of butter; boil together. Add ¼ cup of brandy before removing from fire, then add beaten yolk of 1 egg, and stir in the beaten white just before serving. MRS. O. H. WARD.

SPONGE PUDDING.

Mix thoroughly 2 tablespoonfuls of butter, 4 of sugar, and 4 rounding tablespoonfuls of sifted flour. Wet this

---

VALENTINES VARNISHES **VALENTINE & COMPANY,** Coach and Car Varnishes and Colors

with a part of a quart of milk and put the rest on to boil. When boiling, mix all together, and stir until boiled and thickened. Allow it to become cold, then add 4 eggs, beaten separately. Stir in the yolks first and when well beaten, the whites. Bake an hour, setting into hot water. Delicious with creamy sauce.   MRS. E. M. DUNBAR.

INDIAN PUDDING.

Wet 1 cup of corn meal with part of 3 pints of milk and put the rest on to boil. When boiling, add the meal and stir until it thickens. Remove, put in 1 cup of New Orleans molasses and a tablespoonful of cinnamon with 1 tablespoonful of salt. Pour this mixture into a buttered dish, add 2 cups of cold milk and bake 4 hours in a slow oven.   MRS. D. H. CHAMPLIN.

SPANISH CREAM.

One pint of sweet milk, 1 large spoonful of gelatine dissolved in the milk, 3 eggs, 3 tablespoonfuls of sugar. Beat the yolks of the eggs and the sugar together, and stir in the milk. Cook as for a custard, being careful not to cook too long and take from the fire. Beat the whites of the eggs to a stiff froth, and add to the custard. Season as desired and turn into a mould till cold. Whip cream and turn over the custard, when ready for the table.
     MRS. C. W. CRARY.

POTATO PIES.

One pint of mashed potatoes, 3 eggs, beaten separately, sufficient milk to make a thin batter, the juice and rind of 1 large lemon, a wineglassful of brandy and a large piece of butter. Bake with under crust only enough for 2 large pies. Salt to taste.   M. L. BYLLESBY.

CHARLOTTE RUSSE.

One pint of cream, before it is whipped, whites of 2 eggs, 1 tablespoonful of sugar put in the whites of eggs and whipped cream, ½ teaspoonful of vanilla. Line the dish with lady fingers.   MRS. NEELD.

GINGER SHERBET.

One-fourth pound of sugar, put on to boil in a pint of water. Chip the rind from 3 lemons and 1 orange. Add to the sugar; boil 5 minutes and set away to cool. To the remaining rind and juice of the fruit, add the juice of another lemon; mix with the cold syrup, strain and freeze. Pound 4 ounces of preserved ginger to a smooth paste and press through a sieve. Cut 2 ounces into small bits; mix altogether and stir with 1 tablespoonful of ginger syrup into the frozen ice. Repack.

ORANGE PUDDING.

Beat the whites of 5 eggs very stiff, add 5 tablespoon-

VALENTINE & COMPANY,
Coach and Car Varnishes and Colors

fuls of powdered sugar, ½ level teaspoonful of cream of tartar, ½ saltspoonful of salt and the pulp of 2 large oranges last. Serve with whipped cream or custard.

E. W. E.

LEMON PIE.

PASTRY FOR ONE PIE.

A heaping cup of pastry flour, 1 saltspoonful of Cameo baking powder, 1 saltspoonful of salt, from ⅓ to ½ a cup of butter and lard mixed. Mix the baking powder and salt with the flour, rub in the shortening and mix quite stiff with ice water. For the filling: Mix 1 tablespoonful of corn starch, 1 cup of sugar, ½ saltspoonful of salt and add to 1 cup of boiling water; boil 5 minutes. Add juice of 2 lemons; when cooked a little add yolks of 2 eggs and 1 tablespoonful of butter. Beat the whites stiff with 2 tablespoonfuls of powdered sugar. Pile on the pie and brown. E. A. S.

JELLIED PEACHES.

One dozen good sized peaches, ½ box of gelatine, 1½ cups of sugar, 1½ pints of water. Soak gelatine in ½ cup of water until soft, then put the sugar and the rest of the water in a stewpan and boil five minutes. Put the peaches in and cook 10 minutes, in taking the stew pan from the fire turn the gelatine into it, then add a tablespoonful of good brandy. Set in a dish of cold water to cool, and stir gently once in awhile to keep the peaches from settling at the bottom. When beginning to set put into a mould and put on ice. Serve with whipped cream.

Mrs. T. J. Hudson.

CHAFING DISH.

As that historic barque, long known as Noah's Ark,
  Was filled with choice samples of fowl, flesh and fish;*
So we in modern ages, conning these printed pages,
  Compass like miracles with the Chafing Dish.

*By " poetic license."

MANUFACTURED BY SIMPSON, HALL, MILLER & CO.

LOBSTER A LA NEWBURG.

One large lobster, 1 tablespoonful of butter, 1 wine glass of sherry, 3 eggs, ½ pint of cream. Take the nicest part of the lobster cut in small pieces, put in chafing dish with butter, season with pepper and salt, pour wine over it, add the beaten eggs and cream. Let all come to a boil and serve immediately. Sufficient for five persons.   MRS. JAMES HEWITT.

SCOTCH SQUIRREL.

Spread anchovy paste thinly on crackers. Scramble in the chafing dish, 8 eggs, with 1 cup of cream, a pat of butter, and a little salt. Pour this mixture over the crackers and serve.   MISS ANNIE BENNETT.

CREAMED OYSTERS.

Put into the upper part of the chafing dish 1 tablespoonful of butter. When it melts add 1 tablespoonful of flour; stir till it thickens, then add 1 cup of cream, season with salt and pepper to taste. Add the oysters drained and cook till the oysters are plump. Serve on hot toast.   MISS KATE S. BENTON.

VENISON IN A CHAFING DISH.

One coffee cup of claret; when hot add 1 dessertspoonful of butter, 1 coffee cup of sherry, 1 tablespoonful of currant jelly, 1 dessertspoonful of Worcestershire sauce, a shake of red pepper. When the sauce comes to a boil put in the venison cut in strips five or six inches long, not more than two pieces at a time, and cook for about one minute.   MRS. EBERMAN.

CREAMED OYSTERS.

Mix well together 1 tablespoonful of butter, 3 teaspoonfuls of flour, put in a chafing dish, add a little milk or cream and salt to taste and stir constantly till thoroughly cooked. As it thickens add more milk till a proper consistency is attained. Put in 1 pint of oysters and cook till their edges curl. Serve on toast. This cream is also used for Lobster Newburg.

MRS. ISAAC BENNETT.

OYSTER PAN ROAST.

Melt 1 tablespoonful of butter, and as it creams add 1 dozen large oysters, ½ pint oyster liquor, salt and pepper. Cover and cook about 2 minutes. Put 6 of the oysters on a thin slice of toast on a hot plate, with sufficient liquid to moisten the toast, and serve. MRS. C. H. BIXBY.

PANNED OYSTERS.

Put into a chafing dish a heaping tablespoonful of butter and 1 of flour. Stir well, then add ½ cup oyster liquor, season, and when very hot add the oysters and cook a very few minutes. Serve on hot buttered toast.

MISS KATE S. BENTON.

Heat in the chafing dish 2 tablespoonfuls of butter, ½ teaspoonful of salt, 1 teaspoonful of lemon juice and 1 of currant jelly. Add to this, slices of cold lamb or mutton and serve hot. If curry is liked add it to taste and serve with boiled rice.

POTATOES RECHAUFFE.

Slice 6 cold boiled potatoes, put them in the chafing dish with 1 tablespoonful of butter and ½ pint cream;

simmer 5 minutes and stir in 1 teaspoonful of lemon juice, pepper, salt and the beaten yolks of 2 eggs. Let it simmer and serve hot.   Mrs. W. H. Wells.

HAM A LA ESPAGNOLE.

Put 1 tablespoonful of butter in the dish and when melted, a thick slice of ham. Brown well and remove, mix with the fat in the dish 2 tablespoonfuls of very fine bread crumbs, ½ gill good cider, pepper and a little chopped parsley. Put back the ham, serve when hot.
    Mrs. Atkinson.

CREAMED SHRIMPS.

Cook together 2 tablespoonfuls of butter and 1 of flour with 1 pint of milk until smooth. Add 1 can of shrimps, salt and paprika; simmer until heated through and serve. Lobster may be cooked in the same manner, adding the juice of ½ a lemon.   Miss Longmire.

LOBSTER WITH VINEGAR SAUCE.

Boil 2 eggs 20 minutes. Put lobster in the blazer with a cup of vinegar and water, ½ cup of butter, salt and pepper. Cook until heated through; add the eggs cut in slices; serve.

OYSTERS A LA POULITTE.

Cook together 1 pint of cream, 1 tablespoonful of butter and 1 of flour, stirring constantly. Put in 30 oysters and cook 5 minutes; add salt, pepper and 3 grates of nutmeg. Serve on toast. MRS. ADELAIDE G. WALTER.

KIDNEYS WITH BACON.

Split lamb kidneys in half and skewer them open with wooden toothpicks. Cook in the blazer 6 thin slices of bacon, draw to one side and put in the kidneys. Cook 6 minutes, turning often, until brown and tender; add to the gravy 1 teaspoonful of Worcestershire sauce and serve a slice of bacon on toast with each portion of the kidney and a little gravy. MRS. C. H. BIXBY.

SWEETBREADS SAUTE.

Parboil and blanch the sweetbreads; cut them in ½ lengthwise and each ½ into 2 pieces. Sprinkle with salt and pepper, beat an egg with 1 tablespoonful of water and dip the slices first in this, then in cracker dust and brown in the blazer with 2 tablespoonfuls of butter.
MRS. D. H. CHAMPLIN.

CALF'S LIVER SAUTE.

Heat 2 tablespoonfuls of butter in the blazer with 1 teaspoonful of minced onion; add ½ pound of calf's liver, sliced thin, sprinkled with pepper and salt and coated

VALENTINE & COMPANY,
Coach and Car Varnishes and Colors.

thickly with flour. Cook to a light brown, turning often. When done, draw to the side; add 2 tablespoonfuls of sherry and 1 of mushroom catsup; boil up once and serve.

Mrs. Eberman.

CHICKEN A LA VOLAILLE.

One tablespoonful of butter melted in the chafing dish, 1 tablespoonful of flour rubbed smoothly into it; add 1 cup cream and stir constantly until it thickens. Cut 1 cup white chicken meat into dice, and 8 button mushrooms cut in 4 pieces; add a little celery, cut fine.

Mrs. V. N. Jones.

CREAMED OYSTERS.

Melt in a chafing dish 1 tablespoonful of butter; add 1 tablespoonful of flour and stir until smooth. Pour in 1 cup cream and stir until smooth; add salt and pepper and if too thick, a little oyster liquor. Put in 1 pint of oysters and cook until the edges are well curled. About 2 minutes before serving add a small bunch of celery, cut fine.

Mrs G. T. Smith.

MACCARONIED EGGS.

Melt 1 tablespoonful of butter over hot water; add ½ pint milk and stir in 5 eggs, slightly beaten. When they thicken add ½ cup boiled spaghetti chopped into inch lengths, ½ cup button mushrooms, cut in halves, pepper and salt and 1 tablespoonful of chopped parsley. Cook 3 minutes and serve on rounds of toast garnished with parsley.

MRS. A. EMERY.

TOMATOES AND MUSHROOMS.

Two cups canned tomatoes, 1 tablespoonful of bread crumbs, 1 cup sliced mushrooms, 1 tablespoonful of butter, salt and pepper. Put the tomatoes in the chafing dish first, then the bread crumbs and seasoning; cook a few moments; add the mushrooms, heat through and serve on toast.

MRS. J. M. MARSHALL.

Chop fine 4 veal kidneys with ½ pound calf's liver; season with pepper and salt. Heat a piece of butter in a chafing dish, put in the meat and toss about until done. Remove from the fire and stir in the beaten yolk of 1 egg and ½ teaspoonful of lemon juice. Spread on toast and serve.

VEAL KIDNEY SAUTE.

Chop an onion fine and brown in butter. Cut the kidney in thin slices; add salt and paprika, cook until tender and serve with slices of lemon.

SUNFLOWER.

Boil 4 eggs 20 minutes and cool before removing shell.

VALENTINES VARNISHES **VALENTINE & COMPANY,**
Coach and Car Varnishes and Colors

Make a cream sauce with 1 pint of milk, 1 tablespoonful of flour and 1 of butter, rubbed together and stirred into the boiling milk. Add the whites of the eggs, chopped fine. Season with salt and white pepper. Grate the yolks over the top and serve on a green salad dish, which completes the idea of a sunflower.   Miss Helen M. Topping.

BARBECUED HAM.

Cut rather thick slices of cold boiled ham; lay them in the blazer and let them fry. When they begin to crisp, draw to one side of the dish and add 1 teaspoonful of vinegar, small teaspoonful of white sugar, a saltspoonful of mustard and a little pepper. Mix well and cook about 2 minutes.   Mrs. M. W. Hartwell.

VEAL WITH ASPARAGUS TIPS.

Boil 2 eggs 20 minutes; rub the yolks with 1 tablespoonful of butter to a paste, and heat it with ½ pint of milk in the blazer. Stir until blended, then add 2 cups of veal, cut fine, and 1 cup of cooked asparagus tips. Season with salt and pepper and cook 5 minutes, adding the chopped whites of the eggs.   *

CREAMED CHICKEN.

Rub 2 tablespoonfuls of butter and 1 large one of flour together, add 1 cup of milk or cream and 1 cup of chicken stock. Cook over hot water until smooth; add 2 cups of cold chicken, cut fine, with salt and white pepper. Cook 3 minutes and serve. A little chopped parsley is an addition.
   Mrs. J. B. Daniels.

CREAMED POTATOES.

Make a sauce of 2 tablespoonfuls of butter, 1 of flour, and ½ pint milk; season with salt and pepper. When thick and smooth add cold boiled potatoes, cut into cubes. Heat through and serve hot. This should be done in the blazer set into hot water.   MISS HARPER.

DEVILLED TOMATOES.

Cut the tomatoes into thick slices, without peeling and fry in butter. Keep them hot while adding to the butter in the blazer 1 tablespoonful of butter, 1 of vinegar, 1 teaspoonful of onion juice, 1 of sugar, ½ each of made mustard and salt and a little papsika. Put in drop by drop the beaten yolks of 2 eggs, stirring all the time. Lay the tomatoes in and serve hot.   MRS. CHARLES INGRAM.

SHAD-ROES SAUTE.

Cook the roe 10 minutes in boiling salted water with 1 teaspoonful of vinegar, throw them in cold water for a few minutes, then roll them in flour. Put 2 tablespoonfuls of butter in the blazer and lay in the roe, cut into several pieces. Cook until done. Serve with melted butter and slices of lemon.   MRS. A. G. WALTER.

CREAMED SALMON.

Prepare a sauce of 1 tablespoonful each of butter and flour, stirred smoothly into 1 cup of milk. Add 1 can of

VALENTINES VARNISHES **VALENTINE & COMPANY,** Coach and Car Varnishes and Colors.

salmon, freed from bones and skin. Season with salt, papsika and minced parsley.
Miss Atkinson.

RECHAUFFE OF TURKEY.

Make a sauce of 1 tablespoonful of butter and 1 of flour with ½ pint of stock. Stir until well blended, add small slices of turkey meat, salt, paprika and 2 tablespoonfuls of sherry wine. Cook 2 minutes longer and serve.
Mrs. A. E. Taylor.

EGGS A LA ITALIENNE.

Melt 1 tablespoonful of butter in ½ pint of milk. Stir in 5 eggs, well beaten, and when they begin to thicken, add ½ cup of boiled spaghetti, chopped, ½ cup of mushrooms, sliced, 1 tablespoonful of minced parsley, salt and paprika to taste. Cook 3 minutes and serve.
Mrs. J. B. Wheatley.

STIRRED EGGS.

Melt 1 tablespoonful of butter in the blazer, add 1 gill of brown gravy or stock; when hot, stir in 5 eggs beaten, salt and pepper, also 1 tablespoonful of minced parsley.

CREAMED EGGS.

Beat together 1 gill of chicken or veal stock, 1 of cream, salt and pepper. Beat 4 eggs; add; stir until thick. Serve.

FRICASSEE OF DRIED BEEF.

Put into the blazer over hot water $\frac{1}{2}$ pint of milk, 1 tablespoonful of butter and 1 cup of dried beef, chopped fine. Cook 5 minutes and add very slowly 2 well beaten eggs. Stir until thick and serve on toast. A FRIEND.

CHICKEN WITH MUSHROOMS.

Make a sauce over hot water of 2 tablespoonfuls of butter, 1 of flour with $\frac{1}{2}$ pint of milk and 1 gill of mushroom liquor, add 1 pint of cold chicken. Cook 3 minutes, put in $\frac{1}{2}$ cup of canned mushrooms, sliced. Cook 2 minutes longer and add very slowly the yolks of 2 eggs, salt and pepper, stirring all the time. Serve as soon as the same is smooth. MRS. M. W. HARTWELL.

WELSH RAREBIT—No. 1.

Melt 3 parts of butter in a chafing-dish, then add 1 coffeecup of grated cheese, 3 tablespoonfuls of beer, 1 teaspoonful of prepared English mustard, salt to taste. Stir constantly. When completely melted add two well beaten eggs. Cook one minute and serve on hot buttered toast.
MRS. I. M. BENNETT.

WELSH RAREBIT—No. 2.

Melt ½ tablespoonful of butter in the chafing-dish and when very hot add ½ pound of American cheese, grated,

VALENTINES VARNISHES VALENTINE & COMPANY, Coach and Car Varnishes and Colors.

and a little imported ale. As it cooks and shows a tendency to stick to the dish, add more ale until the mixture is smooth and velvety. Add a heaping teaspoonful of paprika, and when creamy put a spoonful of it on hot toast. Hot plates are absolutely necessary.

Miss Kate S. Benton.

WELSH RAREBIT—No. 3.

One wine glass of cream, 1 pound of New York cheese, 1 teaspoonful of butter, 2 eggs, 1 teaspoonful of Worcestershire sauce. Cut the cheese in small pieces. Put butter in chafing-dish; when melted add cheese and cream. Stir until melted. Add eggs beaten very light, stir all the time and serve on hot toast. Care must be taken that eggs do not curdle.

Mrs. James Hewitt.

OYSTER STEW.

Two tablespoonfuls of bread crumbs and ½ cup of water, cooked for a few minutes. Add 18 oysters and simmer until the edges are slightly curled; add 1 tablespoonful of butter and ½ cup of cream. Season with parsley, lemon juice, salt and pepper.

Mrs. C. H. Bixby.

SCRAMBLED EGGS.

Beat lightly 6 eggs, yolks and whites separately. Then mix and season, adding about ⅓ cup of milk. Cook in upper dish, stirring lightly as it thickens.

Miss Kate S. Benton.

FRESH MUSHROOMS.

Clean and peel the mushrooms, put them in a pan with melted butter and a very small piece of garlic; pepper and salt to taste. Let them cook a few minutes, pour in one cup of sweet cream and let them simmer slowly for ten minutes. Serve very hot.

MRS. B. S. ARNULPHY.

CHICKEN.

A large tablespoonful of butter, stir into it a heaping teaspoonful of flour. Before it browns add ½ cup of white stock, stir a minute, add a little lemon juice, white pepper, salt and ½ cup of cream. Boil up once and add a pint of chicken, cut in small pieces. Reduce the flame and simmer eight minutes.

MISS STANDART.

FROG'S LEGS FRICASSEE.

Put 3 pats of butter in the chafing-dish, when melted add a little salt and 2 teaspoofuls of lemon juice or vinegar. Put in 3 dozen frog's legs, cover the dish and cook 13 minutes but do not burn. Drain off the juice,

VALENTINE & COMPANY,
Coach and Car Varnishes and Colors.

add 1½ cupfuls of white sauce, and if too thick, thin with the juice. Cook three minutes and serve.

L. F. E.

SCRAMBLED EGGS AND SARDINES.

Take 6 eggs and 2 small pats of butter and scramble together. When almost done, add 4 tablespoonfuls of cream and ½ of Worcestershire sauce. Drop in 6 skinned sardines, broken into small pieces.

E. S. W.

SALMON CREAMED.

Into a pint of boiling milk stir slowly 1½ tablespoonfuls of butter, with the same quantity of flour rubbed in, adding ½ teaspoonful of salt, 2 eggs, well beaten, then a pint of cold boiled salmon, broken into pieces. Simmer five minutes.

CREAMED EGGS.

Hard boiled yolks, having half as many bread crumbs as eggs, and half as much cheese, season with salt and pepper, melted butter. Make into balls, put on platter, cover with creamed sauce, sprinkle over with bread crumbs and cheese. Put into oven and brown; seasoned with onion improves. This is a good way to use yolks after making angel cake. MISS STANDART.

CAKE.

If you would have delicious cake,
The greatest care, friend, you must take,
Both how you *mix* and how you *bake*.

Separate beat the eggs, you know,
The whites quite light, to look like snow,
And in the flour, put *Cameo*.

With heat intense, should oven glow,
A pan of cold water will temper it so
That your cake will never burn, ah! no!

A COLONIAL DAME'S RECIPE FOR CONNECTI-CUT LOAF CAKE.

(150 years old.)

Three pounds flour, 2 pounds butter, 2 pounds sugar, 6 eggs, 2 pounds of fruit, raisins and citron, nutmeg to taste, ½ pint wine and brandy mixed. Make sponge over night with ½ pint best yeast, mix in ½ the butter. Mrs. E. L. Hale.

MRS. HENDERSON'S SPONGE CAKE.

Ten eggs, 1 pound pulverized sugar, ½ pound flour, juice and grated rind of ½ a large lemon. Have

VALENTINES VARNISHES   **VALENTINE & COMPANY,**
Coach and Car Varnishes and Colors.

one person beat the yolks with ½ the sugar and another the whites of the eggs for ½ an hour. Then beat the yolks into the whites, stir in lightly the remainder of the sugar, then the flour and lemon by degrees. 1 pound of sugar is 3 cupfuls, ½ pound flour is 2½ cups.

MRS. J. P. MONTROSS.

ENGLISH SEED CAKE.

Stir 1 cake yeast into 1 pint warm milk, rub 4 ounces of butter lightly into 2 pounds flour; add 1 ounce caraway seed, ¼ ounce allspice and ½ pound sugar; add the milk to this, mixing well and kneading into a light dough. Line 2 cake tins with buttered paper, pour in the cake and let it stand in a warm place for more than an hour, then bake in a well heated oven 1½ hours. MRS. J. H. R. BOND.

SUNSHINE CAKE.

Yolks of 11 eggs, 2 cups sugar, 1 of butter, 3 of flour, 1½ teaspoonfuls of Cameo baking powder. Beat the yolks very light, cream the butter and sugar; add flour and baking powder last.

MRS. R. LONGMIRE.

QUEEN OF ALL CAKES.

Bake angel's food in jelly tins, about ½ an inch thick, and allow to become perfectly cold. Whip 1 pint sweet cream, sweeten and add vanilla and 1 pound

almonds, blanched and chopped fine. Spread very thick between the layers. Powdered sugar over the top.
MRS. ANNA W. KNIGHT.

ENGLISH SEED CAKE.

One pound flour, ½ of butter, ½ of sugar, 2 eggs well beaten, ¼ pound seeds (caraway) or ¼ pound raisins and a little candied orange peel; enough milk to make a thin dough. Put into 2 pans and bake 1¼ hours.
MRS. EARL W. SPENCER.

RAISIN CAKE.

One cup brown sugar, ½ of butter, ½ of sour milk, 1½ of sifted flour, 1 of chopped raisins, 2 eggs, or yolks of 4, cinnamon, cloves and nutmeg to suit the taste.
MRS. NEAL.

CUP CAKE.

Four cups flour, 3 of sugar, 1 of butter, 1 of sweet milk, 5 eggs. Flavor with any preferred extract, 3 teaspoonfuls of Cameo baking powder sifted in the flour.
MRS. VIRGINIA M. HARPER.

SPONGE CAKE.

Four eggs, 2 cups sugar, 2 cups flour, ⅔ cup boiling water, 2 teaspoonfuls of Cameo baking powder, lemon.
MRS. S. H. STEVENS.

VALENTINES VARNISHES **VALENTINE & COMPANY,** Coach and Car Varnishes and Colors.

RIBBON CAKE.

Beat together to a cream ½ cup butter and 2 of sugar; add 3 cups flour, into which has been sifted 2 teaspoonfuls of Cameo baking powder; stir in 1 cup milk and the whites of 6 eggs beaten to a froth. Bake in 3 layers and for the middle layer take out 4 tablespoonfuls of the mixture and add to it 1 tablespoonful of molasses, ½ cup flour, 1 cup chopped raisins, ½ teaspoonful of cloves, ½ of soda, 1 teaspoonful of cinnamon and the yolks of 2 eggs. Put this layer between the other 2 with jelly or soft icing and ice the top.

Mrs. J. F. Dickson.

BLACK AND WHITE CAKE.
(Black Part.)

Cream ½ cup butter and 1 of sugar; add ½ cup milk and the yolks of 4 eggs, well beaten; sift 1 teaspoonful of Cameo baking powder with 1½ cup of flour and stir in, then 1 cup chopped raisins, 1 of currants, 1 teaspoonful of cloves, 1 of cinnamon, 1 of allspice and ½ a nutmeg. Bake ½ an hour, then pour over the top the following:

WHITE PART.

Cream ½ cup butter and 1 of sugar; add ½ cup milk and the whites of 4 eggs, well beaten; sift 1 teaspoonful of Cameo baking powder with 1½ cups of flour and add, pour this mixture over the black part and bake until done. Ice with boiled icing.

Mrs. R. Longmire.

POUND CAKE.

Beat 1 pound butter to a cream and add 1 pound powdered sugar gradually. Beat 14 eggs without separating until very light and stir in, beating vigorously; add 1 pound sifted flour, ¼ teaspoonful mace and a wineglass of brandy. Bake 1¼ hours in a moderate oven.

Mrs. F. W. Norwood.

PINEAPPLE CAKE.

Cream ½ cup of butter with 1 cup of powdered sugar, and ¾ cup of milk, 2 cups of flour and 2 tablespoonfuls of corn starch, into which has been sifted 2 heaping teaspoonfuls of Cameo baking powder. Add the whites of 4 eggs, beaten.

Selected.

FILLING.

Beat the whites of 2 eggs to a stiff froth, add 1 cup of powdered sugar and spread between the layers. Drain the juice from a can of pineapples and chop fine, sprinkling it over the frosting. Shell ½ pound of pecan nuts and put them over the frosting. Whip cream with powdered sugar and spread over top and sides

Miss Gertrude A. Hubbard.

VALENTINES VARNISHES — **VALENTINE & COMPANY,** Coach and Car Varnishes and Colors.

FRELINGHUYSEN CAKE.

Cream 1 cup of butter with 1½ of sugar, add 1 cup of molasses, 1 of milk, 4½ of flour, 3 eggs, 1 teaspoonful each of soda, cloves and cinnamon, 1 nutmeg, 2 cups of seeded raisins, and 1 large cup of nut meats, if desired. MRS. A. F. SARGENT.

SPONGE CAKE.

Beat 2 cups of sugar with the yolks of 6 eggs until foamy, add gradually 4 tablespoonfuls of cold water. Beat the whites of the eggs to a stiff froth, add a pinch of salt. Mix all well together with 2 scant cups of sifted flour. Flavor with lemon. MRS. S. W. SEA.

SPICE CAKE.

Mix 1½ cups of brown sugar with 1 of butter, 1 of milk, 3 eggs, 2 heaping teaspoonfuls of Cameo baking powder, sifted with 2½ cups of flour, 1 teaspoonful of cinnamon, a little nutmeg, a pinch of allspice, 1 cup of raisins; vanilla flavoring. Bake in an angel food pan in a slow oven. MRS. EDWARD CARRY.

MRS. GOODRICH'S BERRY CAKE.

Two cups of sugar, scant ½ cup of butter, 1 of milk, 4 of flour, 2 or 3 eggs, 3 teaspoonfuls of Cameo baking powder, 1 box of blueberries or raspberries. Flour the berries and stir in lightly the last thing. Is good hot for tea or cold for lunch. MRS. H. L. HUMPHREY.

NELLIE'S CAKE.

Whites of 8 eggs, 2 cups of sugar, 1 of butter, 3 of flour, 2 even teaspoonfuls of Cameo baking powder, 1 cup of milk. Flavor to taste. Cream the butter and add, alternately, the milk and 2 cups of flour, a little of each slowly. Beat the whites of eggs and sugar together, until smooth, like icing, add flavoring, then the last cup of flour, into which the baking powder has been well mixed, alternately with the eggs and sugar, until all is thoroughly mixed. Bake in a loaf or 2 layers.

MISS NELLIE HARPER.

EGGLESS CAKE.

One and one-half teacups of sugar, ½ of butter, 1 of sour milk, 3 of sifted flour, 2 of chopped raisins, 1 teaspoonful of soda. Cinnamon and nutmeg to taste.

MRS. F. CHAPMAN.

WALNUT CAKE.

Two and one-half cups of flour, 1½ of powdered sugar, ¾ of butter, whites of 6 eggs, frothed, 2 teaspoonfuls of Cameo baking powder, ½ cup of milk, 1 large cup of walnuts.

MRS. F. B. HOOKER.

CARAMEL CAKE.

Boil ½ cake of Baker's chocolate, 1 cup of sugar, ½ of sweet milk and the yolk of 1 egg until it thickens,

VALENTINE & COMPANY,
Coach and Car Varnishes and Colors.

then let it cool. Cream ⅔ cup of butter with 1 of sugar, add the yolks of 2 eggs, beaten, 1 cup of milk, then stir in the above mixture, if cool, then 2½ cups of flour, into which 2 teaspoonfuls of Cameo baking powder have been sifted and 1 teaspoonful of vanilla. Bake in 4 layers.

FILLING.

Boil 2 cups of sugar, a small piece of butter and ⅔ cup of milk 4 minutes, then stir constantly until it thickens. Should it thicken too much add a few drops of milk, until it will spread easily.

MRS. GEORGE MEHRING.

NUT CAKE.

Beat ½ cup of butter and 1½ of sugar to a cream, add ¾ cup of milk and 2 of flour, into which has been sifted 1½ teaspoonfuls of Cameo baking powder. Flavor and add 1 tumbler of nut meats.

MRS. A. G. JONES.

WHITE FRUIT CAKE.

Beat to a cream 1 cup of butter, add 2 cups of pulverized sugar; beat well. Sift into 3 cups of flour 2 teaspoonfuls of Cameo baking powder, add to the creamed butter and sugar, alternately, with the beaten whites of 6 eggs. Bake in jelly cake tins and while hot put between the layers the following filling: Chop fine ¼

CAKE.

pound each of figs, seeded raisins, citron, blanched almonds, and stir them into 3 whites of eggs, well beaten, 1 teacup of powdered sugar and the juice of 1 lemon. Ice the whole with 1 white of egg, well beaten with the juice of ½ a lemon and 1 cup of powdered sugar. MRS. D. H. CHAMPLIN.

ANGEL FOOD FRUIT CAKE.

Use any angel food recipe and bake in jelly tins, not greased. Filling: One-fourth pound candied pineapple and cherries, the pineapple sliced very thin and the cherries halved. Make a boiled icing, flavor with lemon; spread over the cake and lay the fruit upon it.
MRS. MOREHOUSE.

WHITE CAKE.

Cream 1 cup of butter with 2 of sugar, add 1 of milk and 1 cup of flour, not sifted. Beat the whites of 7 eggs and add ⅓ to the mixture, then 1 cup of flour with 1 teaspoonful of Cameo baking powder mixed in it, and another ⅓ of the egg, then mix in lightly the remainder of the egg and another cup of flour. Flavor and bake in a moderate oven. MRS. FLORENCE CHAPMAN.

ORANGE CAKE.

Cream 1 cup of butter with 2 of sugar. Mix 3 even

VALENTINES VARNISHES   **VALENTINE & COMPANY,**
Coach and Car Varnishes and Colors.

teaspoonfuls of Cameo baking powder with 4 scant cups of sifted flour, add 1 cup of milk and the whites of 8 eggs, stiffly beaten.

FILLING.

Boil until quite thick the juice of 4 oranges, 1½ lemons, 8 egg yolks and ¼ pound of sugar rubbed together. Just before removing from the fire add the whites of 4 eggs, well beaten. Let it cool and spread between the layers. Cover with boiled icing and ornament with slices of thinly cut orange. MISS KNAPP.

BANBURY CAKES.

Cut very fine ½ pound fresh candied orange peel, ½ pound candied lemon peel, 1 pound currants, ¼ ounce cinnamon, ¼ ounce allspice, ¼ pound butter, creamed; mix these ingredients well together and keep in glass jar. Make a rich pie crust of 1 heaping tablespoonful lard, 3 of flour, a teaspoonful salt, blend with ice-water, not too wet; cut from this paste round pieces as large as a saucer, put a large teaspoonful of the above mixture in the middle, fold over and pinch the edges together; turn them over, brush with the whites of eggs and dust fine granulated sugar over them. Bake in moderate oven. MRS. BEN WILLIAMS.

CHRISTMAS FRUIT CAKE.

One pound butter, 1 pound sugar, 1 pound flour, 10

common sized eggs or 12 small ones, 2 pounds raisins (stoned), 2 pounds currants, 2 pounds citron (chopped fine), 1 cup molasses, 1 large glass of wine (sherry); spices to the taste. MRS. E. C. LONG.

BLACKBERRY JAM CAKE.

One cup sugar, 1½ cups flour, ¾ cup butter, 1 cup blackberry jam, 3 eggs, 1 teaspoonful soda mixed in cream, 2 whole nutmegs, cinnamon to taste; stir altogether; bake in two layers, with icing between when cold. MRS. A. E. COLEMAN.

CHOCOLATE COFFEE CAKE.

One cup of brown sugar, ½ cup of butter, ½ cup of weak coffee, 1 small teaspoonful of soda, 2 eggs, 2 cups of flour; then grate 1 cup of chocolate, put with half cup of coffee and 1 of brown sugar and 1 yolk egg; cook in a custard boiler and add to the above. Make into layers and use boiled frosting between.

MISS HELEN M. TOPPING.

GRANDMOTHERS' JUMBLES.

One pound flour, ½ pound sugar, ½ pound butter, a little cream, the rind of three lemons with the juice of two, all made into a paste; roll in long rolls size of little finger, then wind round and round till size of ordinary cookies; roll in sugar. MRS. E. L. HALE.

KUCHEN.

Three-quarter pound flour, ½ pound butter, ¼ pound sugar, a little salt; mix well, then roll out and cut with a wineglass; brush each cookie with egg, and sprinkle with sugar and cinnamon before baking.

Mrs. W. H. Benton.

VANILLA WAFERS.

One cup butter, 2 cups sugar, ½ cup cold water, 1 teaspoonful soda, 2 teaspoonfuls vanilla; mix stiff, roll thin and bake quick. Mrs. F. B. Hooker.

SAND CAKES.

Sift 2 cups flour and add 2 cups sugar, break in 2 eggs, add 1 cup butter, mix as soft as possible; roll thin and cut out.

ICING.

Take whites of 2 eggs, add powdered sugar and cinnamon, put 3 blanched almonds on each cake and drop icing in center from spoon; sift flour over the cake tins. Bake and let them stand a few minutes after taking from oven. Mrs. F. C. Swett.

BACHELOR'S BUTTONS.

One and one-half cups of flour, 2 even tablespoonfuls of butter rubbed together, 1 scant cup of sugar, whites of 2 eggs. Divide the dough into pieces the size of walnuts; roll in sugar and bake on paper.

Mrs. W. H. French.

SUGAR COOKIES.

A cup of butter, 2 of sugar, ⅔ of sour milk, with 1 teaspoonful soda dissolved in it; 2 eggs; flavor with nutmeg and caraway seeds; roll granulated sugar on top.   Mrs. J. Y. Scammon.

HERMITS.

Cream together 2 cups of sugar and 1 of butter, add 3 eggs, ½ teaspoonful of soda dissolved in 3 tablespoonfuls of milk, 1 cup of raisins, seeded and chopped, 1 nutmeg, 1 teaspoonful each of cloves and cinnamon, 5 cups of flour; roll out ½ inch thick, cut with round cutter, bake in a quick oven 12 minutes.
Mrs. J. H. Reeves.
Oakland, Cal.

JUMBLES.

One-half pound of butter, 10 ounces of sugar, 12 of flour, 2 eggs, 1 tablespoonful of milk, soda the size of a bean. Save half the sugar to roll the jumbles in and flavor to taste.   Mrs. W. H. Low.

CRULLERS.

One cup of sugar, ½ of butter, ½ of sweet milk, 3 eggs, 2 teaspoonfuls of Cameo baking powder, flour enough to roll out. Fry in hot lard.
Mrs. Virginia M. Harper.

VALENTINES VARNISHES   VALENTINE & COMPANY,
Coach and Car Varnishes and Colors.

DOUGHNUTS.

One cup of sugar, 1 of sweet milk, 2 eggs, 1 tablespoonful of melted butter, 3 teaspoonfuls of Cameo baking powder, a little salt. Roll out as soft as possible.

Mrs. W. H. Low.

CRULLERS.

Cream 2 tablespoonfuls of soft butter and 8 of pulverized sugar, add 3 eggs well beaten, ½ teaspoonful of salt, and 6 tablespoonfuls of milk or 2 tablespoonfuls of milk may be left out and 2 of sherry wine put in. Sift 2 level teaspoonfuls of Cameo baking powder into flour enough to roll out lightly, fry in boiling lard and sift fine sugar over them.

Mrs. E. J. Myers.

MADELINES.

Cream a small cup of butter with 2 of powdered sugar, add 1 cup of milk and sift 3 small teaspoonfuls Cameo baking powder with 2 cups of flour and ½ of corn starch. Beat 4 eggs separately, leaving out 2 of the whites for icing, add with 1 cup of currants and 1 of nut-meats to the cake and bake in small tins. Flavor with almond and vanilla.

Mrs. E. M. Dunbar.

MATILDA'S FRUIT CAKE.

One cup each of sugar, molasses, seeded raisins and milk, 3 tablespoonfuls of butter, 3 eggs, 3½ cups of flour, with 2 teaspoonfuls of Cameo baking powder, 1 teaspoonful of vanilla.

Mrs. Chas. A. Knorr.

CURRANT CAKE.

Cream together 1 cup of butter, 2 of sugar, add 5 eggs, 4 cups of flour, 1 of milk, 1 pound of currants, washed, dried and floured, added the last thing; 2 scant teaspoonfuls of Cameo baking powder mixed with the flour. The grated rind of a lemon and a little almond extract greatly improves the cake. This quantity will make 2 loaves. MRS. HARRY GOWER.

ROCKS.

Mix together like cake 1 cup of butter, 1½ of sugar, 2½ of flour, 2 of raisins chopped, 3 eggs, 1 teaspoonful of cinnamon, 1 of soda in a little warm water, 1 pound of English walnuts broken into small pieces, a pinch of salt. Drop from spoon on buttered tins and bake in quick oven. MRS. HELEN ATKINSON.

FRUIT CAKE.

Four cups of flour, 2 cups of brown sugar, 1 cup of butter, 4 eggs, 1 cup of molasses, 1 cup of sour milk, ½ wineglass of brandy, 1 teaspoonful of soda, 2 tablespoonfuls of cinnamon, 2 of cloves, 2 pounds of raisins, ½ of currants, ¾ of citron, ½ cup of flour to sprinkle over fruit before putting in mixture. Bake 3 hours in moderate oven in a 6 quart pan. MRS. STANDART.

VALENTINE & COMPANY,
Coach and Car Varnishes and Colors.

MY GREAT-GRANDMOTHER'S RECIPES.

WEDDING CAKE.

Three pounds of flour, 3 of sugar, 3 of butter, 6 of currants, 3 of raisins, 2 of citron, 1 ounce of mace, 1 of cinnamon, 1 of nutmeg, ½ of clove, ½ pint of brandy, 2 dozen eggs. Cream butter and sugar, add the eggs, which have been previously beaten, and the brandy. Mix the spice and fruit with flour and stir all thoroughly together. Bake in 6 loaves about 4 hours.

SUGAR GINGERBREAD.

One cup of sugar; ⅔ cup of butter, 2 eggs, ⅓ teaspoonful of soda, ⅔ of cream, about 2 large cups of flour. ginger and vanilla. Rub butter and sugar to a cream and add the eggs and soda dissolved in the cream, also the flavoring. Then knead in flour enough so that it can be rolled out. Roll thin on tin sheets and sprinkle a little sugar on the top.

GINGER SNAPS.

One cup of molasses, ⅔ cup of sugar, ⅔ cup of butter, ⅓ teaspoonful of soda, ½ teaspoonful of ginger, ½ teaspoonful of cinnamon, flour. Stir molasses, sugar and butter together and boil about 3 minutes. Remove from the stove and add the ginger and soda (dry soda). Begin at once to stir in flour with cinnamon added. Stir till the mass can be put upon the moulding board and knead till it can be rolled out smooth and thin. It can be rolled on tin sheets and cut in squares or shapes before baking.

NEW YEAR'S COOKIES.

Three-fourths of a pound of butter, 1 pound of sugar, 3 eggs, 1 cup of sour milk, 1 teaspoonful of saleratus, ½ cup of caraway seed, a little mace, flour. Rub butter and sugar to a cream, add the eggs, milk, saleratus, mace, caraway seeds and flour to make it stiff enough to roll thin. Roll with a little sugar, cut in shapes, and bake about ten minutes. MISS NOYES.

CHOCOLATE CAKE.

Beat until light 1 cup of butter with 3 of brown sugar, add 1 cup of milk and 4 of flour with 3 teaspoonfuls of Cameo baking powder. Put in also the yolks of 7 eggs and 9 tablespoonfuls of grated chocolate. MRS. A. W. P.

CARAMEL CAKE.

Large cup of sugar, ½ of butter, 3 eggs, beaten separately, 2 teaspoonfuls of Cameo baking powder, put into flour enough to make stiff, flavor with vanilla; bake in 3 layers. Filling: Boil 2 coffeecups of "C" sugar with 1 cup of milk and butter the size of an egg until

VALENTINE & COMPANY,
Coach and Car Varnishes and Colors.

waxy, but not too hard; flavor with vanilla, stir until cool and spread between the cakes.

Mrs. J. L. Rhodes.

HICKORY NUT JUMBLES.

One-half pound of butter, ⅔ pound of sugar, 3 eggs, ½ pound of flour, 2 cups of hickory nut kernels, flavor with vanilla; bake in a moderate oven. M. L. B.

FEATHER CAKE.

Two cups of sugar, ½ cup of butter, 3 cups of flour, 3 eggs, 3 teaspoonfuls of Cameo baking powder, juice and rind of 1 lemon. Ice with soft icing and serve with tea or chocolate the day they are made.

Mrs. J. H. Long.

ALMOND LAYER CAKE.

Two cups of pastry flour or 1¾ cups of bread flour, 2 teaspoonfuls of Cameo baking powder, 1 cup of granulated sugar, ½ cup of butter, ½ cup of milk, whites of 3 eggs. Cream butter with hand, slowly, add sugar, then milk, drop by drop, alternating with flour, lastly, the beaten whites of the eggs. Divide mixture into two pans, bake one plain; over the other sprinkle ⅓ cup of blanched sliced almonds, dust over with a little powdered sugar; allow 12 minutes for baking. Filling: One cup of granulated sugar, ⅓ cup of water; boil; white of 1 egg, beaten stiff, beat into mixture, add ⅔ cup of chopped almonds. Mrs. Standart.

BREAD CAKE.

Take 1 cup light bread sponge, mix to it 1 cup of sugar, ¾ of butter, ½ of sour milk, 1½ of flour, 2 eggs, ½ teaspoonful of soda, 2 cups of raisins, spice; let it rise. M. W. S.

ALMOND CAKE.

Beat to a cream 1 pound of powdered sugar and ¼ pound of butter, add 8 eggs, beaten separately and very light; add to 1 pound of flour 2 teaspoonfuls of Cameo baking powder. Blanch and beat fine 1 cup of almonds, with a little rosewater and add a teaspoonful of bitter almonds and 1 wineglassful of brandy.

FIVE CAKE.

Cream 1 cup of butter with 2 of pulverized sugar, add 5 eggs, beaten separately, ⅔ cup of milk, 3 cups of flour and ¼ teaspoonful soda, dissolved in the milk. Flavor with vanilla. L. W. A.

DOUGH CAKE.

Four teacups of raised dough, 2 cups sugar, 1 of butter, 2 of raisins, 4 eggs, spice to taste, 1 wineglass of brandy. Let it rise in the pans, until light. Bake slowly. Mrs. B. Smith.

VALENTINE'S VARNISHES **VALENTINE & COMPANY,** Coach and Car Varnishes and Colors.

COFFEE CAKE.

Cream 1 cup of butter and 1 of sugar, add 1 of molasses, 1 of strong coffee, 2 of raisins, ½ of milk, 1 teaspoonful of soda, 1 quart of flour. Spices.

M. D. E.

SILVER CAKE.

Cream 1 cup of butter with 1 of powdered sugar, add 3 cups of flour, whites of 8 eggs, 2 teaspoonfuls of Cameo baking powder, 24 almonds, blanched and chopped. Flavor with extract of bitter almonds.

GOLD CAKE.

Cream 1 cup of butter with 2 of sugar, add 4 cups of flour, 1 of milk, yolks of 8 eggs, 1 teaspoonful of Cameo baking powder, nutmeg and citron.

Miss Mary E. D.

ORANGE CAKE.

Beat to a cream ½ cup of butter with 2 of sugar, ½ cup of milk, 2½ of flour, 5 eggs, beaten separately. Bake in layers. Take the white of one of the eggs and beat to a stiff froth, beat in powdered sugar and the juice and grated rind of 1 orange, until thick enough to spread between the layers. Miss Nellie H.

HICKORY NUT CAKE.

Cream together ½ cup of butter with 1½ of sugar,

¾ cup of milk, 2 of flour, 2 teaspoonfuls of Cameo baking powder, whites of 4 eggs, 1 cup of hickory nut meats.
Miss Susan J. F.

CITRON CAKE.

Cream 2 cups of butter with 3 of sugar, add 1 cup milk, 5 of flour, 6 eggs, 1 teaspoonful of soda, sliced citron.

SHURDIE CAKE.

Cream 1 cup of butter with 2 of sugar, add 1 cup of milk, 2 eggs, and 4 cups of flour, into which sift 2 teaspoonfuls of Cameo baking powder. Put in 1 tumblerful of nuts and flavor with lemon.
Mrs. J. W. Harrison.

DOUGHNUTS.

Beat together 1 cup of white sugar, yolks of 3 eggs, 1 cup of milk, butter the size of an egg, small teaspoonful of salt, the beaten whites of the eggs, and 3 teaspoonfuls of Cameo baking powder sifted into enough flour to roll out soft. Fry in lard and dust with sugar.
Mrs. J. H. Rhodes.

VALENTINES VARNISHES **VALENTINE & COMPANY,** Coach and Car Varnishes and Colors.

CAKE.

SUGAR COOKIES.

Two cups of sugar, 1 of butter, 2 eggs, ¾ cup of sour milk, level teaspoonful of soda, nutmeg or lemon extract.   Mrs. Roosevelt.

GINGER COOKIES.

Boil up once 2 cups of molasses, ½ of sugar, 1 of butter, 1 tablespoonful of ginger and a little cinnamon. When cool add 2 well beaten eggs and 1 teaspoonful of soda. Mix rather soft with flour and do not roll very thin.   Mrs. Neeld.

RAISED CAKE.

Two heaping cups of raised bread dough, 2 cups of sugar, 1 of butter, 1 of seeded raisins, ½ teaspoonful of soda, lemon extract, cinnamon and nutmeg.

Mrs. Neeld.

FRIED CAKES.

Rub to a cream 1 teacup of sugar and 1 heaping tablespoonful of butter, 3 eggs, beaten separately, 1 coffee cup of sweet milk, 4 teaspoonfuls of Cameo baking powder, put into flour, and flour enongh to roll out very soft.

Miss Clara Williams.

CONFECTIONERY.

Roly-poly, isn't he fat?
Plump as a peach, yes, more than that;
Candy was his hourly cry,
Candy was his bosom's sigh.

CREAM PATTIES.

The whites of 2 eggs beaten, 2 tablespoonfuls of cold water. Stir in sifted confectionery sugar slowly until stiff enough to mould in patties. Flavor with peppermint, vanilla, wintergreen or chocolate. To color them pink for wintergreen flavoring, use the juice from stewed cranberries.

MISS HARRIETTE A. RICHARDSON.

MARSHMALLOWS.

One-half pound white gum arabic dissolved in 1 pint of water and add ½ pound fine sugar, place over the fire until it thickens; add the whites of 4 eggs beaten stiff. Flavor with vanilla, pour in tins, sprinkle lightly with corn starch.

VALENTINES VARNISHES VALENTINE & COMPANY, Coach and Car Varnishes and Colors

CHOCOLATE CARAMELS.

One and a half pounds of sugar, 1 teaspoonful of vanilla, ¼ pound "Baker's" chocolate, ¼ pound butter, 1 cup cream. Grate the chocolate and put it on the stove with the cream; stir the sugar in gradually, then add the butter, boil well for 10 minutes and add 1 teaspoonful of vanilla before taking off the fire.

Mrs. E. A. S. Clark.

FUDGES.

One and a half pounds pulverized sugar, ¼ pound "Baker's" chocolate, ¼ pound butter, 1 teaspoonful of vanilla, 1 cup cream. Grate the chocolate, add the cream, then the butter and sugar. Boil until the mixture is thick, stirring frequently; before removing from the fire, add the vanilla. Pour into a buttered pan and cut in squares.

Mrs. W. H. Benton.

VASSAR FUDGES.

Boil, stirring constantly, 2 cups granulated sugar, 1 of milk, butter the size of an egg, ½ cake "Baker's" chocolate, until the spoon parts the boiling candy so that the bottom of the chafing dish can be seen; add 1 tablespoonful of vanilla and stir until nearly stiff, pour into buttered pans and mark into squares. Miss Katharine Smith.

FUDGES.

Put into a saucepan 2 cups of sugar, 1 of milk, a piece of butter as large as an English walnut and ¼ cake chocolate cut fine. Boil 20 minutes, add 1 teaspoonful of vanilla; stir in a cool place until stiff; put into buttered pans an inch thick and cut into squares.

MISS EVADNAH WILLIAMS.

PEANUT CANDY.

Melt 2 cups sugar, stirring constantly; add 1 cup chopped peanuts; pour into shallow pans to cool and cut in squares or long pieces. MISS LOUISE GREGG.

BUTTER SCOTCH.

Boil 1 cup sugar, ½ of water, 3 tablespoonfuls of vinegar and 1 of butter until it becomes brittle in water.

MISS LOUISE GREGG.

CHOCOLATE CARAMELS

Boil 1 cup molasses, 1 of brown sugar, 1 of milk, butter the size of an egg, 1 tablespoon of glycerine; when nearly done add 1 cup "Baker's" unsweetened chocolate, grated. Test it in cold water. Pour into buttered tins and when cool cut into squares. MRS. A. W. KNIGHT.

CONFECTIONERY.

COARSE CARAMELS.

Three cups light brown sugar, 1 of milk, ⅓ of butter, 4 squares "Baker's" chocolate. MRS. JAMES HEWITT.

MOLASSES CANDY.

Boil 2 cups molasses, 1 of sugar, 1 tablespoonful of vinegar and 1 of butter until it becomes hard in water. When nearly done add a pinch of soda. Pour into shallow tins and when cool, pull until a light brown color.
MISS LOUISE GREGG.

CREAM CANDY.

Two cups of sugar, 1 cup of water, 1 teaspoonful of butter, 1 small teaspoonful of cream tartar, 1 teaspoonful of vanilla. Boil without stirring until it will harden in cold water. After taking from the stove stir in the vanilla and turn out on a greased platter. Begin to pull as soon as you can handle it. MRS. RHODES.

NUT CANDY.

Two cups of New Orleans molasses, ¾ cup of brown sugar, 1 coffeecup of walnut meats. Boil sugar

VALENTINE VARNISHES VALENTINE & COMPANY, Coach and Car Varnishes and Colors.

and molasses until it will harden quickly in water. Add a piece of butter and walnut meats just before removing from fire. Pour in shallow pans to cool.

CREAM CARAMELS.

Two cups of light brown sugar, ½ cup of sweet cream. Let this boil hard 5 to 10 minutes, then beat it to a cream; add vanilla. Pour into a buttered pan, flatten out and cut in squares.

COCOANUT CANDY.

Two cups of cocoanut, 1 cup of sugar, 2 tablespoonfuls of corn starch, whites of 2 eggs. Mould in little balls and put on buttered paper. Dry in a slow oven.

MAPLE SYRUP CANDY.

Two cups of maple syrup, ¼ teaspoonful of cream of tartar, ½ of vanilla, 1½ cups of hickorynut meats. Boil the syrup and cream of tartar till a little of the syrup dropped in cold water will form a ball in the fingers. Remove from the fire and cool. When lukewarm stir till it becomes creamy, add the vanilla and nuts and pour immediately into a buttered tin pan. It

VALENTINE'S VARNISHES **VALENTINE & COMPANY,** Coach and Car Varnishes and Colors.

is better to have the candy at least ½ inch in thickness when poured out in the pan. MISS NOYES.

WHITE TAFFY.

Two pounds of sugar, 1 pint of water, ¼ teaspoonful of cream of tartar, vanilla. Boil sugar, water and cream of tartar till, when tested in cold water, it will snap. Pour out on buttered marble slab to cool. Drop a little vanilla on the top and when it has cooled sufficiently to make it white and glossy, pull into strips and cut into small pieces. MISS NOYES.

CREAM PEPPERMINTS.

Three pounds of granulated sugar, 1 cup of water, ¼ teaspoonful of cream of tartar, oil of peppermint. Boil sugar, cream of tartar and water rapidly till, when a little is dropped in cold water, it will just form into a soft ball in the fingers. Be sure not to stir the syrup after it has commenced to boil or it will grain. When the "soft ball" will form, remove instantly from the fire and allow it to become lukewarm. Then stir with a wooden paddle, always in the same direction, adding a few drops of oil of peppermint, until it has become per-

VALENTINE & COMPANY,
Coach and Car Varnishes and Colors.

fectly smooth and creamy. If the candy grains water can be added and it can be boiled again. Drop on parafine paper, a marble slab or plate of glass.

CREAM WINTERGREENS.

These are made the same as the peppermints, except that oil of winter green is substituted for oil of peppermint. MISS NOYES.

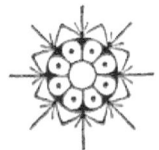

PICKLES AND PRESERVES.

CANNING FRUIT.

If fruit you jelly, preserve or can
Take care that you *skin* it, close as you can,
See that *every bubble* is out of the jar,
If those are left in, they, the best fruit, will mar;
Follow close this rule and there is in reason
Why you can't have fresh fruit at every season.

WORCESTERSHIRE SAUCE.
(Genuine.)

Two ounces of cayenne pepper pods, 2 ounces of white mustard seed, 2 ounces of ground cloves, ¼ ounce of ground mace, 1½ pounds of shalots, 4 cents worth of garlic, ¼ pound of horse radish, 1 gallon of brown vinegar. Mix all together in a jar, stirring every day for a month; boil and strain. It will be fit for use in a week.

MRS. C. G. F. WELLS.

CUCUMBER SAUCE.

Take 36 large, green cucumbers, 4 large, white onions, peel and chop fine; add 1½ cups of fine salt and let them drain 8 hours in a hair sieve. Then add ½ cup of black

VALENTINE & COMPANY,
Coach and Car Varnishes and Colors.

mustard seed, ½ cup of black pepper; mix well together, put in a stone jar, and cover with hot cider vinegar. After standing a week, drain several hours, and cover with fresh boiling vinegar. Put in Mason jars and seal while hot.

Mrs. B. R. Wells.

TOMATO BUTTER.

Four pounds of ripe tomatoes, 4 pounds of brown sugar, 1 pint of vinegar, ground spices to taste, cinnamon, cloves and allspice. Peel and heat the tomatoes; when softened press through a colander, add the other ingredients and boil until thick. Very nice with meats.

Mrs. J. F. Dickson.

TOMATO SOY.

One peck of tomatoes peeled, 1 quart of vinegar, 1 pound of sugar, 1 even teaspoonful of ground cloves. Boil down one-half.

Mrs. C. G. L. Kelso.

GOOSEBERRY CATSUP.

Nine pounds of gooseberries, 6 pounds of sugar, 3 quarts of vinegar; boil the fruit alone and strain, add sugar and vinegar, with cloves, cinnamon and allspice to taste; boil one hour.

Mrs. S. H. Stevens.

VALENTINES VARNISHES VALENTINE & COMPANY, Coach and Car Varnishes and Colors.

SWEET GREEN TOMATO PICKLES.

Eight pounds of tomatoes, 2 pounds of sugar, 3 pints of good cider vinegar, 1 ounce of cloves, 1 ounce of cinnamon, ½ ounce of allspice, ½ ounce of mace, ¼ of a teaspoonful of salt. Chop the tomato and cook it a few minutes, (it may be cooked by steaming) scald the spices and sugar in the vinegar and pour upon the tomato.

Mrs. H. L. L. Ladd.

CHOW CHOW.

One-fourth of a peck of green tomatoes, ¼ of a peck of white onions, ¼ of a peck of pickling string beans, 1 dozen large, green peppers, 1 large head of cabbage, 1 pound box of mustard, ¼ of a pound of white mustard seed, 1 ounce of celery seed, ½ ounce of turmeric, ½ ounce of cinnamon, 4 tablespoonfuls of black pepper, 2 pounds of sugar. Chop the vegetables, remove the seeds from the peppers, sprinkle each layer with salt, let it stand over night, then strain and rinse in clear water. Put in a porcelain kettle a layer of vegetables and a layer of spices; cover with the best cider vinegar and boil 20 minutes. Can be used immediately.   Mrs. Walter R. Comstock.

MANDRAM.

Equal parts of onions, cucumbers and green peppers (without seeds) served with a French dressing.

VALENTINES VARNISHES VALENTINE & COMPANY,
Coach and Car Varnishes and Colors.

PICKLES AND PRESERVES.

CHILI SAUCE.

Twenty-four large, ripe tomatoes, 10 medium sized onions, 3 large red peppers, 10 small long peppers, 5 tablespoonfuls of salt, 5 tablespoonfuls of sugar, 2 tablespoonfuls of cinnamon, 1 large tablespoonful of celery salt, 1 teaspoonful each of cloves and allspice, 1 ounce of mustard seed, 7 cups of vinegar. Chop onions and peppers, skin the tomatoes, boil 2 hours.   MRS. HARRY GOWER.

ORANGE MARMALADE.

Slice 13 large oranges and 5 lemons very thin, removing the seeds and about ½ the rind of the oranges, cover with water and let it stand 36 hours; then boil slowly 4 hours, add 7 pounds of sugar and boil 20 minutes.

MRS. S. A. HOUSTON.

PARISIAN APPLE SAUCE.

Boil until soft 1 pound of finely sliced apples, 1 gill of water, 1 ounce of butter, grated yellow rind of ½ a lemon, 2 bay leaves, 2 ounces of sugar, pass through a sieve, stir in 1 tablespoonful of orange flower water and 1 of apricot jam.   MRS. B. B. BRYAN.

CUCUMBER AMD ONION PICKLES.

Chop and salt separately 25 cucumbers and ½ peck of onions. After 24 hours squeeze out the brine and cover

VALENTINE & COMPANY,
Coach and Car Varnishes and Colors.

with weak vinegar over night. Drain and pack in layers in stone jar, sprinking upon the layers mustard and celery seed, with whole cloves, until the jar is full. Cover with good vinegar over night. In the morning drain and heat the vinegar with 2 cups of brown sugar. Pour hot upon the pickles. Do this twice before storing.

Mrs. Chas. A. Knorr.

TOMATO CATSUP.

Boil 1 bushel of tomatoes until soft, put them through a fine wire sieve, add 2 quarts of vinegar, 1 pint of salt, 2 tablespoonfuls of cloves, ¼ pound of allspice, 2 ounces of cayenne pepper, 3 tablespoonfuls of black pepper, 3 quarts of onions boiled soft enough to rub through a sieve, 5 heads of garlic, skinned and separated. Mix all together and boil about 3 hours or until reduced one-half. Bottle without straining.

Mrs. George H. Cook.

TOMATO CONSERVE.

Gently boil 3 pounds of tomatoes with 3 pounds of sugar for 3 hours, adding 2 lemons, peeled and sliced thin, the peel cut into bits, and 2 inches of preserved ginger root cut very fine.

H. M. W.

VALENTINE'S VARNISHES   VALENTINE & COMPANY,
Coach and Car Varnishes and Colors.

WATERMELON PICKLES.

Cut the pared rind into thick slices, put into large stone jar and cover with boiling water in which is just enough powdered alum to make it pretty bitter—an ounce at least. Let it stand several hours on back of stove, take out into cold water, and when cold boil a half hour in syrup, or till tender. Syrup—8 pounds of fruit, 4 pounds of best brown sugar, 3 pints of vinegar, 1 cup of mixed whole spices, stick of cinnamon, cloves and allspice (less of cloves). Tie the spices in a bag and boil with the sugar and vinegar; skim well and add fruit.

MRS. S. H. STEVENS.

PICKLED WATERMELON RIND.

Pare off the thin green rind, cut the white in pieces, cook in clear water until tender, take from the water and drain. To 1 quart of good cider vinegar add 3 pounds of sugar, 4 ounces of cinnamon, and 2 ounce of cloves (tie the spices in a muslin bag), boil five minutes, put in the melon and boil fifteen minutes. MRS. H. L. L. LADD.

NEW YORK CUCUMBER PICKLES.

Make a brine of 1 pint of salt to 1 gallon of water, and pour boiling hot over small cucumbers, and let them stand

VALENTINES VARNISHES VALENTINE & COMPANY, Coach and Car Varnishes and Colors.

twenty-four hours. Rinse and drain the cucumbers, and pack in glass jars. In each jar put a small piece of horse-radish, a small white onion, and a teaspoonful each of black and white mustard seed, celery seed, and juniper berries. Fill the jars with boiling vinegar, and seal quickly. To each gallon of vinegar allow ½ a pound of sugar.

Mrs. A. L. Guion.

A good recipe for canning peaches, apricots and berries is to make a syrup of equal parts of sugar and water. *Skim well* and put in all the fruit it will hold. Cook slowly till tender.

Cotton batting tied over fruit in stone jars, while hot, makes a good air-tight covering.

A glass of claret added to a kettle of peaches just before taking them from the fire, gives them a delicious flavor.

SPICED GRAPES.

Seven pounds of Malaga grapes, seeded, 4 pounds of sugar, 1 pint of vinegar, 1½ teaspoonfuls each of ground cinnamon, cloves and allspice. Make a syrup of the vinegar, sugar and spices (put in bags). After skimming *thoroughly* put in the grapes and cook till tender.

Mrs. J. J. Reeves,
Redlands, Cal.

VALENTINES VARNISHES **VALENTINE & COMPANY,** Coach and Car Varnishes and Colors

PICKLES AND PRESERVES.

APPLE-BANANA JELLY.

Boil crabapples in a little water till thoroughly tender; strain the juice through a flannel bag and boil twenty minutes. For each glass of syrup add a glass of sugar and boil five minutes, or till jellied. Pour out In a pitcher and add Burnett's banana flavoring to taste. Pour into glasses and set to cool.

APPLE-STRAWBERRY JELLY.

Use apples as above and add strawberry flavoring instead of banana.
Mrs. W. E. Reeves,
San Bernardino, Cal.

ONE-TWO-THREE JAM.

One pint of currant juice, 2 pounds of ripe currants, 3 pounds of raisins, 4 pounds of sugar, 6 oranges. Seed raisins and chop fine; chop rather fine the peel of four of the oranges. Cook all together until soft.
Mrs. J. H. Rhodes.

SWEET PICKLE PEARS.

Boil 10 pounds of pears until soft, using good solid fruit. Make a syrup of 2 pounds of sugar, 1 quart of vinegar. Pour out fruit and can in glass. Mrs. Rhodes.

BEVERAGES.

GRAPE JUICE.

Wash and pick from the stems 14 pounds of grapes and put them in a kettle with 1 pint of water; scald enough to extract the juice, stirring occasionally; squeeze and strain, add 1 quart water and 3 pounds sugar; scald 5 minutes and bottle at once; scald the corks until thoroughly swelled, drive them in level with the bottle, and seal airtight. MRS. A. P. MOORE.

FRUIT PUNCH.

Squeeze and strain 6 oranges and 4 lemons, add ½ can of grated pine apple, sugar to taste and fruit coloring to make it pink; add nearly a gallon of water, but in doing this the juiciness of the fruit must govern. Make this in the morning to use at night. MRS A. P. MOORE.

GINGER ADE.

Dissolve 3 pounds loaf sugar in 2 gallons water, add the well-beaten whites of 3 eggs and 2 ounces of ground Jamaica ginger moistened with a little water; bring slowly

---

VALENTINES VARNISHES **VALENTINE & COMPANY,**
Coach and Car Varnishes and Colors.

to the boiling point, skim and settle; when cold, add the juice of a large lemon and ¼ yeast cake, dissolved in 2 tablespoonfuls warm water; mix, strain, bottle, tie the corks down and in two days it is ready for use.

MRS. F. FAIRMAN.

CLARET CUP.

One bottle of claret, juice of 3 or 4 lemons, a dash of Jamaica rum; Apollonaris water. MRS. J. Y. SCAMMON.

CURRANT CORDIAL.

Pour 1 quart best whiskey upon 1 pound bruised currants and 1 ounce white ginger root, bruised; let it stand 24 hours, then strain through a flannel bag; add 1¼ pounds loaf sugar, and bottle when the sugar is dissolved; excellent for a chill. MRS. G. A. SODEN.

CLARET PUNCH.

Juice of 3 lemons, 1 teacup of sugar, 1 coffee cup of made black tea, drawn cold, 1 orange peeled and sliced thin, one lemon peeled and sliced thin, 2 strips of cucumber rind added, for 30 minutes before serving and then removed; 1 quart best claret, 1 quart of Apollinaris water or champagne; ice.

MRS. C. M. PEPPER.

CIDER PUNCH.

Mix 1 cup of sugar, ½ of water and 1 of sherry wine; slice in 2 lemons, stir until the sugar is dissolved and add 1 quart best cider.   H. M. W.

RASPBERRY SHRUB.

This should be made of very ripe berries. Soak 3 quarts of berries in 1 of pure cider vinegar for 24 hours; strain, and add to liquid 3 quarts fresh berries; after 12 hours strain again and boil 20 minutes, adding 1 pound sugar to each pint of the liquid. Bottle, and when using, put one tablespoonful in each glass of water.

    Mrs. J. W. Harrison.

CHOCOLATE.

Put into the double boiler 3 pints rich milk; when it comes to a boil stir in ½ pound grated chocolate; continue stirring constantly for five minutes at least; beat the yolks of 3 eggs thoroughly and pour the boiling chocolate upon upon them, stirring all the time; add 1 teaspoonful whipped cream to each cup when served.   Mrs. H.

VALENTINE & COMPANY, Coach and Car Varnishes and Colors.

VIRGINIA EGG NOG.

Beat thoroughly the yolks of 8 eggs with 1 pound granulated sugar; add ½ gal. fresh, rich milk, pour upon it very slowly, and stirring briskly, 1½ pints best Jamaica rum; beat the whites of the eggs with a little pulverized sugar to a stiff froth; stir into the whole and finish with a finely grated nutmeg.

CREAM BEER.

Boil together for five minutes 2 ounces tartaric acid, 3 cups white sugar, juice of 1 lemon and 1 quart of water; when nearly cold add the whites of 3 eggs, well beaten, ½ cup of flour and ½ ounce wintergreen essence; bottle and keep cool; when served, put 3 tablespoonfuls in a glass of ice water; add a little baking soda and drink while foaming
F. W.

GINGER BEER.

Slice a lemon, bruise ½ ounce ginger root, 1½ pounds white sugar, 1 ounce tartaric acid, 2½ gallons water, boiled and poured over the ingredients; when cool add a yeast cake and let it stand in a warm place for twelve hours; bottle and tie down the corks; use in two days.
Mrs. Lockwood.

VALENTINE & COMPANY, Coach and Car Varnishes and Colors.

LOWLE.

One half dozen lemons, ½ dozen oranges, 1 pint of claret, 1 gill of brandy, sugar to taste. Cut the oranges in slices and squeeze the lemons and put in sugar, then 1 quart of chopped ice; let stand in cold place until ready for use, and then add claret and brandy.

Mrs. C. A. Williams.

FRUIT PUNCH.

Juice of 6 lemons, juice of 3 oranges, ½ of a pineapple, chopped very fine, ½ cup of strawberries, chopped ice, sugar to taste.

STEAMED BATTER PUDDING.

One egg, 1 cup of milk, 1½ of flour, pinch of salt, 1 teaspoonful of Cameo baking powder, 1 tablespoonful of meled butter. Mix thoroughly, put in pudding dish and steam 20 minutes.

SAUCE.

One-half cup of butter, 1 of pulverized sugar, 1 tablespoonful of cream; stir until very light. Stir into this 1 quart fresh strawberries. Let stand one hour and serve on hot pudding.

PICKLED PEACHES.

One pint of vinegar, 3 pounds of sugar to 1 gallon of fruit. After fruit is cooked boil the syrup until thick; cinnamon and cloves. Use cling peaches, pare and remove seed.

SPICED GOOSEBERRIES.

Five quarts of gooseberries, 3 pounds of brown sugar, 1 pint of vinegar, 1 teaspoonful of ground cloves, 1 teaspoonful of ground cinnamon. Pick berries out and boil altogether ¾ of an hour. Take out the goose-

berries and boil to a syrup ¼ of an hour longer. Serve with roast meats. MRS. RHODES.

GINGER COOKIES.

One egg, 1 cup of sugar, 1 cup of molasses, 1 cup of shortening, part butter and part lard, 1 tablespoonful of soda, 1 tablespoonful of ginger, 1 tablespoonfu of vinegar. Flour to roll. Roll thin.

MRS. C. C. BEATTY,
Redlands, Cal.

CHEESE WAFERS.

One cup of butter, 2 cups of flour, 1 cup of grated cheese, salt and cayenne pepper in water. Take puff paste, roll out, and spread with above mixture, fold over, roll out again, cut into any shape desired, and bake in a quick oven. MRS. J. W. ELEMING,

FRUIT FRITTERS.

Make a batter of 1 egg, 1 teaspoonful of Cameo baking powder, a pinch of salt, a little milk and flour to make

VALENTINE VARNISHES VALENTINE & COMPANY, Coach and Car Varnishes and Colors.

stiff batter. Dip each piece of cooked fruit in the batter and fry in butter to a golden brown.

Mrs. E. L. Houston,

PERFECTLY WHITE DRESSING.

White of 2 eggs, juice of 2 lemons, 2 tablespoonfuls of water. Heat lemon juice and water, stir in the well-beaten whites of eggs and beat continually with Dover beater while cooking. When it looks like white custard, stir in a tablespoonful of butter and season to taste.

Kate D. Fleming.

EGG GEMS.

Mix together chopped meat and bread crumbs, with butter, pepper, salt, and a little milk. Fill some buttered gem pans with the mixture, break an egg carefully over the top of each, sprinkle some very fine cracker crumbs over the top. Bake 8 minutes.

BAKED CABBAGE.

Cook cabbage until tender, drain, cut fine and bake in a buttered pan, covered with a white sauce and buttered bread crumbs. Bake until the crumbs are brown.

VALENTINES VARNISHES VALENTINE & COMPANY, Coach and Car Varnishes and Colors

FRENCH BEEF ESSENCE.

One half pound of chopped lean beef, ½ pint of lukewarm water, 4 drops of muriatic acid. Put all together in a glass fruit jar, cork tight, shake every 15 minutes for 3½ hours, then strain, season with salt and pepper to make it palatable, keep in cool place. Dose, ½ teaspoon hourly, and more, if patient desires.

Mrs. H. P. Knapp.

RASPBERRY FLOAT.

Whip the whites of 4 eggs stiff, add ¾ of a cup of powdered sugar, beat well, then add 1 cup of raspberry jam and beat with a spoon for 40 minutes. Pile on a glass dish and serve with whipped cream.

Mrs. Rhodes.

FLOOR POLISH.

One quart of boiled linseed oil, ½ pint of turpentine, ½ pint of shellac. Mix well and put on hardwood floor with a flannel cloth.

Mrs. Rhodes.

PROPER GARNISHES.

With roast beef or veal serve horse radish.
With roast mutton currant jelly.

VALENTINE & COMPANY,
Coach and Car Varnishes and Colors.

MISCELLANEOUS.

With boiled mutton, caper sauce.
With roast pork, apple sauce.
With boiled chicken, egg sauce.
With roast lamb, mint sauce.
With roast turkey, oyster sauce.
With Venison, or duck, black currant jelly.
With boiled fresh mackerel, stewed gooseberries.
With boiled trout, butter sauce.
With compote of pigeons, mushroom sauce.
With fresh salmon, green peas with cream sauce.
With roast goose, apple sauce.

THINGS WORTH KNOWING.

Rubbing tough meat with cut lemon.
Bacon fat for frying chicken or game.
Dipping sliced onions in milk before frying.
Heating crackers before using.
Heating dry coffee before making.
Pouring vinegar over fish before scaling.
Fried sweet apples with liver and kidney.
Putting a little lemon juice into the water in which rice is boiled.

VALENTINE & COMPANY,
Coach and Car Varnishes and Colors.

MISCELLANEOUS.

RAISIN ROLL.

Mix with milk until soft enough to roll out, 2 cups of flour, into which 2 teaspoonfuls of Cameo baking powder has been sifted, 2 tablespoonfuls of butter and a pinch of salt. Spread with a mixture of 1 cup of raisins, seeded, the grated rind and juice of a lemon ½ cup of sugar. Steam 1 hour and eat with sauce.

Mrs. B. F. Ray.

FRUIT SUET PUDDING,

One teaspoonful of soda, ½ teaspoonful of salt, ½ saltspoonful of cinnamon, ½ of nutmeg sifted into 2½ cups of flour; rub in ⅔ cup of butter and 1 of chopped suet, add 1 cup of chopped raisins and currants. Mix 1 cup of milk (or water) and 1 cup of molasses, stir it into the dry mixture. Steam 3 hours in a buttered mould.

Miss Edith A. Stevens.

LEMON TARTLETS.

The grated rind and juice of 2 lemons, ½ pound of granulated sugar, 2 well beaten eggs, and a large tablespoonful of butter, melted. Mix well and bake in puff paste in pate pans. This makes 1 dozen tartlets.

Mrs. H. Geower.

VALENTINE & COMPANY,
Coach and Car Varnishes and Colors.

PLAIN PLUM PUDDING.

Two cups of *very fine* bread crumbs (of bread a day old) pressed down, ½ cup of flour, 1 cup of suet, 1 of chopped apple (also very fine) 1 cup of stoned raisins, ½ cup of currants, 1 of sugar, rind and juice of a lemon, a little candied peel and 3 eggs. Work well together and steam 4 hours. Mrs. H. Grower.

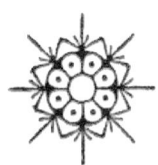

HOUSEHOLD HINTS.

Darn table cloths with linen ravelings.

It is healthful to drink a glass of water before breakfast.

Here is a recipe for one of the best, if not the best, tooth powder obtainable:

TOOTH POWDER—Take one ounce of powdered borax, two ounces precipitated chalk and one ounce powdered castile soap.

An excellent domestic remedy for sore mouth and sore throat is a weak solution of borax and water used freely.

A solution of borax and soda used as a gargle for the throat and mouth, and as a wash for the face, neck, hands and arms, when going out and on returning to the house, and especially when visiting the sick, is considered very efficacious in warding off contagious diseases.

A solution of borax and soda will remove tan.

VALENTINES VARNISHES **VALENTINE & COMPANY,**
Coach and Car Varnishes and Colors.

A weak solution of borax makes an excellent wash to remove dandruff.

Washing the mouth and teeth frequently with a weak solution of borax tends to sweeten the breath.

A piece of borax the size of a pea allowed to dissolve slowly in the mouth will greatly relieve the hoarseness caused by colds, or by long speaking or reading aloud.

To cleanse nursing bottles and tubes, wash them in weak borax water. If two are used—which is the best plan —keep the one not in use full of weak borax water.

To starch collars, cuffs, shirt bosoms and fine muslins so that they will look like new, add to each quart of made starch one-half teaspoonful of borax and a tiny bit of butter or lard.

To keep ants from the pantry sprinkle powdered borax upon the shelves.

To remove the shiny look common to some complexions add a pinch of borax to the water in which the face is bathed.

VALENTINE & COMPANY,
Coach and Car Varnishes and Colors.

A pinch of borax added to the water in which infants are bathed tends to strengthen the skin and prevent chafing.

A weak solution of borax is highly recommended as a wash for sore eyes, redness of the edges of the lids, etc.

A weak solution is excellent as a healing lotion for slight cuts and scratches.

The strength of the solution may vary somewhat, according to the purpose for which it is to be used. A teaspoon level full of powdered borax to a pint of water is not too strong for most uses; but for infants and very small children it may be made weaker.

Mothers will experience much relief from the burning and smarting of the nipples, caused by baby's nursing, if they will wash the nipples at once in borax water.

To soften and whiten the hands bathe them in hot, soft water, to which a good sized pinch of borax has been added.

To remove the odor of perspiration, dust powdered borax—with a powder puff—under the arms after bathing.

VALENTINE & COMPANY,
Coach and Car Varnishes and Colors.

Carpets may be kept clean by going over them once a week, with a broom dipped in hot water, to which a little turpentine has been added. Wring a cloth out in the hot water and wipe under the pieces of furniture which are too heavy to be moved.

To take varnish, paint or pitch from cotton goods, apply oil of turpentine. Wash off in soap suds.

For neuralgia oil of peppermint will usually relieve the pain; wet it in well, but do not get it near the eyes.

Kerosene will soften boots and shoes which have been hardened by water, and render them as pliable as new.

Ripe tomatoes will remove ink and other stains from the hands.

Keep the teakettle bright by rubbing with kerosene and polishing with dry flannel.

GOLD MEDAL OIL POLISH—Twelve pounds Spanish whiting, one-half pound of light brown English castile soap, three ounces aqua ammonia, two ounces olive oil, one ounce

VALENTINES VARNISHES VALENTINE & COMPANY, Coach and Car Varnishes and Colors.

sassafras oil, one pint soft, warm water. Shave the soap fine and dissolve in part of the water, add both of the oils and the ammonia. Mix well with the hands, put in half of the whiting—which must be sifted through a flour sieve Mix thoroughly with the hands, and add the rest of the whiting gradually and the water very sparingly, until all the whiting has been worked in. You may think, for awhile, that it is not going to mix and a little more water may be necessary, for it will be very crumbly; but if you keep at work it will gradually soften and mix all right. When you get it into a solid mass, knead it on a board like bread dough. Roll it out about an inch in thickness, cut into cakes any size desired and put on a board in a dry place, till thoroughly dry, then pack in a box. The above will cost you about 75 cents; and will make twenty-five good sized cakes. So you see it would not cost you more than 3 cents per cake.

STUFFED APPLES—Shell and blanch twenty-four al monds. Chop them fine. Seed and chop a quarter of a pound of raisins. Measure and pick over a half cup of dried currants. Put the almonds, raisins and dried cur

VALENTINE & COMPANY,
Coach and Car Varnishes and Colors.

rants into a saucepan, add a half cup of water, a half cup of sugar, with a teaspoonful of lemon juice, and the grated rind of the lemon. Simmer gently for at least thirty minutes. In the meantime, pare and core six large apples, keeping them perfectly whole. Stand them in a baking pan, sprinkle over about two tablespoonfuls granulated sugar, and bake slowly until the apples are tender and slightly brown. Take from the oven, put them in a glass dish Now, boil the fruit mixture and syrup together for at least ten minutes; that is, boil it hard. Take it from the fire, fill in the spaces from which the cores of the apples have been taken, and baste the syrup over the outside. Stand away to cool. When ready to serve, heap around the outside of the dish, banking it up towards the apples, cream whipped to a stiff froth. Dust the whole with powdered sugar and serve.

To prevent cake from burning, set a pan of water in the oven.

Put a lump of butter in a pan, and when it begins to brown add a little chopped onion. Cut veal kidneys in

VALENTINE & COMPANY,
Coach and Car Varnishes and Colors.

slices and saute them until a light brown. Eat with lettuce, dressed with French dressing.

To remove the tops of fruit jars that cannot be started by hand, dip a cloth in very hot water and apply to the outside of the cap. This will cause it to expand.

A little lemon juice stewed with prunes adds flavor to them.

Always boil maccaroni, tapioca, etc., before putting them into soup.

Soak gelatine in cold water; dissolve it in boiling water.

TESTIMONIALS.

After giving the Cameo Baking Powder a fair test, I do not hesitate to say that hereafter in our family we will use no other, when Cameo is to be had.

MRS. IRWIN SIMPSON.

I cheerfully recommend Cameo Baking Powder.

MRS. H. L. HUMPHREY.

We use Cameo Baking Powder and like it very much.   MRS. G. W. HOYT.

The best baking powder which I have ever used.

MRS. J. B. DANIELS.

After using Cameo Baking Powder, I have decided to use no other. It gives perfect satisfaction.

MRS. W. H. FRENCH.

I have used Cameo Baking Powder, and find it equally good with Royal or Price's.

MRS. JOS. GREGG.

TESTIMONIALS.

Cameo is carrying the day in our family. We use no other.
Mrs. W. F. Parish.

I have used Cameo Baking Powder, and found it equal, if not superior, to all others.
Mrs. Chas. A. Knorr.

For making cake, biscuit, etc., I find Cameo Baking Powder excellent. Have given it a good trial. I cheerfully recommend it.
Mrs. R. Longmire.

I cheerfully recommend Cameo Baking Powder.
Mrs. J. F. Marshall.

I have used Cameo Baking powder with good success, and am glad to recommend it.
Mrs. C. H. Bixy.

Cameo is exactly as good as any other baking powder, and much cheaper.
Mrs. V. M. Harper.

The lightest and whitest of biscuits and the best of cakes are made with Cameo.
Mrs. F. A. Neal.

TESTIMONIALS.

Use Cameo if you want the best results.

Mrs. F. H. Waite.

Have found the Cameo Baking Powder as good, if not better, than any I have ever used.

Mrs. C. H. Ingram.

VALENTINES VARNISHES   **VALENTINE & COMPANY,** Coach and Car Varnishes and Colors.

HUSBANDS.

"Sirs, respect your dinner, idolize it, enjoy it, and you will be many hours in the week, many weeks in the year, and many years in your life, happier."

A RECIPE FOR COOKING HUSBANDS.

One of the lecturers before the Baltimore Cooking School recently gave this recipe for cooking husbands:

"A good many husbands are utterly spoiled by mismanagement. Some women go about as if their husbands were bladders, and blow them up. Others keep them constantly in hot water. Others let them freeze by their carelessness and indifference. Some keep them in a stew, by irritating ways and words; others roast them. Some keep them in a pickle all their lives. It cannot be supposed that any husband will be tender and good, managed in this way, but they are really delicious when they are properly treated.

"In selecting your husband, you should not be guided by the silvery appearance, as in buying a mackerel, nor in the golden tint, as if you wanted a salmon. Be sure to select him yourself, as tastes differ. Do not go to the market for him, as the best are always brought to your door. It is far better to have none, unless you will patiently learn how to cook him.

"A preserving kettle of the finest porcelain is best, but if you have nothing but an earthenware pipkin, it will do, with care. See that the linen in which you wrap him is nicely washed and mended, with the required number of buttons and strings tightly sewed on. Tie him in the kettle by a strong silk cord called Comfort, as the one called Duty is apt to be weak.

"Make a clear steady fire out of Love, Neatness and Cheerfulness. Set him as near this as seems to agree with him. If he sputters and fizzes, do not be anxious,—some husbands do this till they are quite done. Add a little sugar, in the form of what confectioners call kisses, but no vinegar or pepper, on any account. A little spice improves him, but it must be used with judgment. Do not stick any sharp instrument into him to see if he is becoming tender. Stir him gently, watching the while, less he lie too flat and close to the kettle, and so become useless You cannot fail to know when he is done.

"If thus treated, you will find him very relishable, agreeing nicely with you and the children, and he will keep as long as you want, unless you become careless and set him in too cold a place."

HOUSEHOLD HINTS.
(CONTINUED.)

HOME ENGRAVING ON GLASS.

Spread the place with melted parrafine. When hard, trace through it the desired design. Then pour over it hydrochloric acid; allow it to remain about 20 minutes. Wipe all off, when it will be prettily done. Desirable for glove or handkerchief boxes.

REMEDY FOR WHOOPING COUGH OR SEVERE COLD.

One tablespoonful of cod liver oil, 1 tablespoonful of glycerine, 2 tablespoonfuls of honey, wineglass of whiskey. Shake well and give at any time cough comes on as often as needed. MRS. E. L. HALE.

FOR CLEANING SILVER.

Dissolve 1 pound cyanide of potassium in 2 gallons of water. Dip the silver in and wipe off immediately. It should be added to this, that the above is a deadly poison.

MAPLE SUGAR ICING

Scrape the sugar, put it into a granite pan and stir

until hot. To each ¼ pound allow 1 tablespoonful of boiling water. If it seems too thick, add more water.

CURIOUS EFFECTS OF CAMOMILE.

A decoction of the leaves of common camomile will destroy all species of insects, and nothing contributes so much to the health of a garden as a number of camomile plant dispersed through it. No greenhouse or hothouse should ever be without it, in a green or dried state; either stalks or flowers will answer. It is a singular fact, that if a plant is drooping and apparently dying, in nine cases out of ten, it will recover, if you plant camomile near it.

A DELICIOUS GRUEL.

Boil 1 tablespoonful of rolled oats in a pint of water, adding more water if necessary, with a small pinch of salt. When the oatmeal is thoroughly cooked, put through a strainer; to the jelly thus obtained, add ½ cupful of sweet cream and the whites of 2 eggs that have been beaten stiff, as for frosting; sweeten and flavor to taste; if nutmeg or vanilla is used, be careful to flavor delicately.

K. B. D.

TURKISH PILAF.

One cup of stewed, strained tomatoes, 1 cup soup stock highly seasoned with salt, pepper, and minced onion. When boiling add 1 cup of cooked rice, stir lightly till the liquor absorbs it, then add ½ cup of butter. Set it on the back of the stove in double boiler for 20 minutes. This is used as a vegetable.

ORANGE TARTLETS ARE TEMPTING.

Orange tartlets make a dessert which the young people are sure to appreciate. Take the juice of 2 Havana oranges and the grated peel of 1; ¾ of a cup of sugar or ½ cup if the oranges are very sweet; 1 tablespoonful of butter, the juice of ½ a lemon to wet 1 teaspoonful of corn starch. Beat all well together and bake in tartlet shells without cover.

FOR QUICK FREEZING.

Place the preparation to be frozen in a tin pail set in bucket containing a weak solution of sulphuric acid and water; into this throw a handful of Glauber's Salts and freeze rapidly.   Mrs. James Hayes.

SOUTHERN WAY OF COOKING RICE.

Wash a cup of rice in several waters until the milky look is gone. Have ready a kettle full of boiling water (3 or 4 quarts), salted. Put in the rice and stir until the water boils again that it may not stick to the bottom. Keep up the hard boiling until a grain feels soft between the fingers. Strain the water off and serve in a hot dish. Every grain having had room to "kick" will be separate.

Mrs. A. W. Knight.

DRESSING FOR TURKEY.

Use the crumb of a loaf of bread, ½ a grated onion, ½ cup of melted butter, a pinch of sage, salt and pepper to taste. This makes a dry dressing; if preferred moist, add a little milk.   Mrs. J. L. Van Uxem.

PLUM STUFFING.

Chop 2 large apples fine, 3 handfuls of bread crumbs, ½ cup of raisins, ½ of currants, 1 of pitted prunes, 1 tablespoonful of cinnamon, 1 of melted butter; sugar to taste.   MRS. BEN WILLIAMS.

Scratches on varnished wood may often be removed by laying a coarse cloth, saturated with linseed oil, over them, allowing it to remain awhile; polish with a dry flannel.

HOW TO SERVE CHEESE SALAD.

Even an epicure will not scorn a well-made cheese salad. Here is one of the most attractive ways in which it may be served:

Use cream cheese and mix with it a very little green coloring paste. Then roll the cheese into balls the size of birds' eggs. This can be easily done by using the back or smooth side of butter-pats. Get fresh young lettuce leaves; wet them with French dressing and arrange on a flat plate in little groups to look like nests. Into these nests put a few cheese balls and serve out one to each guest.

COUGH MIXTURE.

Half an ounce of antimonial wine, the same quantity of stick licorice and glycerine, 1 ounce of paregoric, 1 of gum arabic, 5 cents' worth of rock candy, dissolved in 1 quart of water. One tablespoonful four times a day is a dose for an adult.   MRS. S. H. STEVENS.

MEMORANDUM.

The cook deserves a hearty cuffing
Who serves roast fowl with tasteless stuffing,
For fowls, like women, are at their best
When well and *seasonably* dressed.

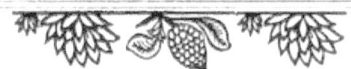

" O, hour of all hours, the most blessed upon earth.
Blessed hour of our dinners!

LILLIAN RUSSEL, ✧ ✧ TRADE MARK.
MADAME NORDICA,
Isadore Rush, Della Fox,
Marie Jansen, Josephine Knapp,
And many others noted for beauty,
use and endorse
Patented May 31, 1894.

Madame Ise'bells
TURKISH BATH OIL AND TOILET PREPARATIONS
FOR THE COMPLEXION.

MADAME ISE'BELLS Retail Parlors for Facial Treatments, Hair Dressing, Shampooing, Manicuring and Chiropodist Work, Removed to

15 East Washington St., Suite 42,
Over French & Potters. In Woman's Club B'ld'g.

By mentioning this advertisement, you can obtain consultation on facial blemishes and a trial treatment of Turkish Bath Oil without charge.

Armour's ✧ Star ✧ Ham

Is always Branded in the Skin as shown in cut.

Nothing Finer can be Produced.

ARMOUR'S ★ STAR
BREAKFAST BACON,
SELECTED AND SLICED.

Guaranteed the Choicest Selection from Young and Healthy Pork.

PERFECTION IN CURE AND FLAVOR.

For sale in **one-pound boxes** by leading Grocers and Marketmen.

The Bacon can also be obtained in strips from 4 to 6 lbs. each.

We may live without poetry, music and art;
　　We may live without conscience, and live without heart;
We may live without friends; we may live without books;
　　But civilized man cannot live without cooks.

We may live without hope,—what is hope but deceiving?
　　We may live without love,—what is passion but pining?
But where is the man that can live without dining?

BLACKALL'S BEST COFFEE,

2¾ Lbs. for $1.00

DOUBLE CONE COFFEE POTS,

105 Madison Street, - - CHICAGO.

G. C. KNAUSS,
Grocery and Market
BEST HAM AND BACON
IN MARKET.
Michener Bros. & Co.'s
5141-5143 LAKE AVE.

We have Removed to
30 WASHINGTON ST.
Opposite Marshall Field & Co.
The Cleanfast Hosiery Co.
E. W. Peck, Mgr.
CHICAGO. NEW YORK.
SPECIALTIES: HOSIERY, UNDERWEAR, BABIES' SHOES.

T. VAN CRAENENBROECK. F. VAN CRAENENBROECK.

University Haberdashers,

Latest Styles of Hats and Gents' Furnishing Goods,

346 FIFTY-FIFTH ST.

AG'TS FOR A. G. SPALDING & BROS.' SPORTING GOODS.

C. L. RAIFF & CO.
Grocery ⁑
and Market,
124-126 35th Street.

GRUBB'S
CUT RATE DRUG STORE,
Cor. Lake Ave. and 53d St.
Department Store Prices.
FINEST SODA WATER IN HYDE PARK.

TESTIMONIAL.

The distinguishing feature of the stove on the opposite page is its excellent broiler, superior to any we have ever used—unsurpassed for steaks, chops, or toast.

Mrs. J. B. Daniels.

www.ingramcontent.com/pod-product-compliance
Lightning Source LLC
Chambersburg PA
CBHW020239170426
43202CB00008B/140